KU-303-731

THE NURSE'S MATERIA MEDICA

THE NURSE'S
MATERIA MEDICA

JOHN GIBSON
MD, FRCPsych

FIFTH EDITION

**BLACKWELL
SCIENTIFIC PUBLICATIONS**
OXFORD LONDON EDINBURGH
BOSTON MELBOURNE

© 1965, 1970, 1973, 1976, 1980 by Blackwell Scientific Publications
Editorial offices:
Osney Mead, Oxford, OX2 OEL
8 John Street, London, WCIN 2ES
9 Forrest Road, Edinburgh, EHI 2QH
52 Beacon Street, Boston, Massachusetts, USA
214 Berkeley Street, Carlton, Victoria 3053, Australia

First published 1965
Second edition 1970
Third edition 1973
Fourth edition 1976
Reprinted 1978
Fifth edition 1980

Typeset by Enset Ltd
Midsomer Norton, Bath
and printed and bound
in Great Britain by
Butler & Tanner Ltd
Frome, Somerset

DISTRIBUTORS

USA
Blackwell Mosby Book Distributors, 11830 Westline Industrial Drive, St Louis, Missouri 63141

Canada
Blackwell Mosby Book Distributors, 120 Melford Drive, Scarborough, Ontario, MIB 2X4

Australia
Blackwell Scientific Book Distributors, 214 Berkeley Street, Carlton, Victoria 3053

British Library Cataloguing in Publication Data

Gibson, John, b. 1907
The nurse's materia medica.—5th ed.
1. Drugs
I. Title
615′.1′024613   RM125

ISBN 0–632–00685–4

Preface to Fifth Edition

For the fifth edition this book has been revised throughout. Twenty-eight new drugs have been added, and a number of little used or superseded drugs removed.

I am indebted to Mr D. Scarr, M.P.S. for the help he has given in the preparation of this edition.

Contents

How to Use This Book

This book is intended to help nurses, trained and in training, to understand the drugs they may have to administer to their patients. The nurse should refer to it for information about any drug of whose dose, actions and effects she is uncertain.

Names. One drug may have several names. Of these, one is the official British name. Other names for the same drug may be in common use; and in America the official name may be slightly different from the British one. After these names, in this book, are given some of the proprietary names. These proprietary names are the property of particular firms. A proprietary name should always begin with a capital letter. Proprietary names are usually easier to spell and pronounce than official names and are therefore in common use.

The nurse may find herself having to administer a proprietary preparation in which more than one drug is combined. In some of these preparations, drugs of similar action are combined, in order that a small dose of each can be given. In other preparations, two drugs may be combined in order that any undesirable effects produced by one may be counteracted by the other.

Dose. If the nurse is worried by the dose prescribed, she can check it here. The doses given in this book are the official ones or ones commonly ordered. The nurse should appreciate that a doctor is not bound to give the official dose, but may order more or less of any drug at his discretion. If the nurse finds, on studying the dose of the drug given here, that a doctor has ordered a much bigger dose, she should check that the doctor really did intend to order a big dose and she should find out why.

Doses for children are usually smaller than doses for adults. On p. xi the nurse will find guidance on smaller doses for children.

Method of Administration. Unless otherwise stated, the drug is intended to be given by mouth. If the drug is to be given in any other way (e.g. by injection) or when the nurse might feel some doubt, she will find the method of administration stated.

Action and Uses. The nurse should study the actions and uses of any drug that she has to administer in order to understand why it is being used. Drugs are grouped in sections according to the use for which they are chiefly used.

Toxic and Side Effects. The nurse should refer to these passages in the book if a patient appears to develop any undesirable reactions after taking a drug. These reactions may be the result of an over-dosage; they may indicate that the patient is particularly sensitive to the drug; or there may be unavoidable side-effects if the drug is given in effective doses. The nurse will find guidance here as to whether the effects are serious or not and whether it is safe or not to continue to administer the drug.

Abbreviations

BP   —blood pressure
kilogram   —kilo
microgram   —mcg
milligram   —mg
gramme (gram)   —g
millilitre   —ml
microcurie   —μc
millicurie   —mc

Metric System Equivalents

250 mg = 0.25 g
500 mg = 0.5 g
1 000 mg = 1.0 g
1 000 mcg = 1 mg
1 000 ml = 1 litre
1 μc = 1 millionth of a curie
1 mc = 1 thousandth of a curie

Weights

A kilogram (kilo) = 2.2 lb
A person's weight in kilos is his weight in lb divided by 2.2.

Doses for Children

In this book, except where otherwise stated, the dose of a drug is that usually given to an adult. Children are usually given much smaller doses. The *Percentage Method* is one way of estimating the dose for a child. In this method the dose for a child is the following percentage of the adult dose.

Approx. age	Weight kilo	lb	Per cent of adult dose
Birth	2.5	5½	10
	3.2	7	12.5
2 months	4.5	10	15
4 months	6.5	14	20
12 months	10	22	25
18 months	11	24	30
5 years	18	40	40
7 years	23	50	50
10 years	30	66	60
11 years	36	80	70
12 years	40	88	75
14 years	45	100	80
16 years	54	120	90

The nurse will see that by this method a child of 12 months is given a quarter the adult dose, a child of 7 years is given half the adult dose, and a child of 12 years is given three-quarters the adult dose.

For further information on drugs and doses for children, the nurse is referred to: Catzel P. *The Paediatric Prescriber* (Blackwell).

Controlled Drugs

The officially-termed in Britain Controlled Drugs are certain drugs especially liable to cause addiction, such as opium, morphine, cocaine, pethidine and diamorphine (heroin).

The nurse should know this about them:

a Stocks of Controlled Drugs can be obtained for a ward from the Pharmacy only by a written, signed order of the Sister or Nurse in Charge.

b A special order-book is kept for Controlled Drugs, and a copy of each order must be kept by the Sister or Nurse in Charge.

c The Controlled Drugs must be kept in a special locked cupboard (usually within the Schedule D Poisons cupboard). The Sister or Nurse in Charge must carry on her person the key to this cupboard.

d The doctor ordering a Controlled Drug to be given must write on the patient's medicine card the full amount or the number of doses of the drug to be given and must sign the order.

e A record must be kept in the Controlled Drug Register of all Controlled Drugs received in the ward and of each dose given. Each dose is signed for by the nurse who gives it and by a second nurse who checks that the drug and dose are correct. Any drug wasted is also entered and signed for by the two nurses.

f The stock of Controlled Drugs in a ward and the Register are checked regularly by the hospital pharmacist.

Prescription Only Medicines

These were formerly called Scheduled Drugs
These drugs are not considered to be as dangerous as the Controlled Drugs and are not so strictly controlled.

The nurse should know this about them:

a Prescription Only Medicines (Scheduled Drugs) are supplied to a ward only on the written order of a doctor or dentist or of the Sister or Nurse in Charge.

b They must be kept in a locked Poison Cupboard, the key of which is held by the Sister or Nurse in Charge.

c Individual doses of these drugs are not recorded in any special register.

d Poisons for external use are stored in a separate poison cupboard kept solely for them. The bottles are grooved so that the nurse can identify them by touch.

e The hospital pharmacist will inspect the cupboard regularly to check the contents and see that the regulations are being observed.

Administration of Drugs

The administration of drugs to patients is an important part of a nurse's work.

Drugs are administered:

a by mouth: for absorption from the mouth or from the small intestine;

b by injection: by subcutaneous, intramuscular or intravenous injection;

c by other methods: into the nose for absorption by the nasal mucous membrane, by spray for absorption by the lungs, through the skin, into the rectum, by local injection into joints, etc.

The commonest ways are by mouth and injection.

Administration by mouth

Most drugs are given by mouth. It is the easiest way to take a drug, but it does not guarantee that the drug is absorbed. The absorption of a drug depends upon a number of factors, especially:

a the amount of the drug in a tablet or capsule: the amount of active ingredient is about 10 per cent, the rest being the medium, the inert substance with which it is combined by the manufacturer;

b the size of the particles of the active ingredient in a particular preparation of it;

c the presence or not of food in the stomach;

d the rate of absorption of the active ingredient by the small intestine;

e the speed of gastrointestinal movement: a reduction in speed gives the drug more chance of absorption, diarrhoea reduces absorption;

f the presence of any gastrointestinal disease which interferes with the absorption of drugs as well as of food (e.g. any malabsorption syndrome);

g any interaction in the gastrointestinal tract between two or more drugs taken at the same time.

Some drugs (e.g. insulin) are ineffective if given by mouth as they are destroyed in the stomach. Others (e.g. aspirin) irritate the mucous membrane of the stomach. Some are manufactured with an 'enteric coating' around them; this coating is not dissolved until the drug arrives in the small intestine, the drug being in this way protected from the acid gastric juice and the mucous membrane of the stomach being protected from any irritant action of the drug.

Taken on an empty stomach, a drug is usually absorbed in 1–2 hours. Taken on a full stomach, it is absorbed more slowly. When slow absorption of a drug is required, it can be administered in a special 'sustained release' capsule.

Once a drug has been absorbed by the cells of the mucous membrane of the small intestine, it passes into the portal venous system and is transported to the liver. Some drugs are chemically changed in the liver. From the liver the drug passes into the general circulation and is transported in the blood throughout the body.

Drugs given by injection

Drugs are given by injection:

a subcutaneously: when slow absorption is necessary;
b intramuscularly: when rapid absorption is necessary, the blood-supply of muscles being richer than that of the skin;
c intravenously: when rapid absorption is necessary.

The form of the drug has to be such that it is absorbable in one of these ways. Some drugs (e.g. insulin) can be given only by injection. Some drugs (e.g. fluphenazine), although administered intramuscularly, are prepared in such a way that they are slowly absorbed over several weeks.

In shock, when the peripheral blood-supply is reduced, drugs are not absorbed when given subcutaneously and only slowly when given intramuscularly.

Transport in the body

Having passed into the general circulation either through the liver (when taken by mouth) or directly (when given by injection), a drug is carried in the blood plasma. But not all the drug is available to the tissues in an effective form. The plasma contains proteins and some of the drug becomes 'bound' to these proteins and ineffective. Only the drug that is not bound is effective. The amount of the drug in the plasma is affected by the amount of available plasma protein to which it could become bound: in some diseases it is reduced and some of it may already have become bound to some other drug the patient has just taken.

The 'target organ' is the tissue or micro-organism the drug has to reach to become effective. Antibacterial drugs have to be taken up by bacteria, digitalis has to be taken up by heart muscle cells, antiepileptic drugs by cells of the brain, and so on.

Excretion

After acting on a tissue or micro-organism, a drug is returned to the blood and so back to the liver. There a drug may be chemically changed. The ability of the liver to deal with a drug can be reduced by disease of the liver or by the action of other drugs on it.

From the liver many drugs pass in the blood to the kidneys to be excreted in the urine. A dangerous accumulation of a drug in the blood can occur if repeated doses of it are taken when kidney function is impaired by disease.

The dose of a drug

The dose of a drug is decided by the doctor who prescribes it. It may be:

a the official or generally agreed dose, as found out by previous clinical trials on patients;

b individually selected by the reaction of a patient to it, e.g. by testing the blood pressure after a dose of an antihypertensive drug or the blood sugar after a dose of insulin;

c controlled by the estimation of the plasma-level of the particular drug in the patient.

Estimation of the plasma-level of a drug can be used to find the optimal dose of a drug that is being given regularly. It is commonly used with:

antibiotics	anticonvulsants
antidepressants	digoxin
warfarin	levodopa

salicylates in the treatment of rheumatic fever.

Response of a patient to a drug

The response of an individual patient to a drug can vary because:

a the severity of a patient's illness can affect his reaction to a drug;

b the 'target organ' can react differently to a drug in different people;

c the rate at which people react to a drug can vary with the size of the dose of the drug;

d fat or large people react less than thin or small people to the same dose;

e disease of the gastrointestinal tract, liver or kidney may interfere with the absorption, action or excretion of the drug;

f some people develop tolerance to a drug by having frequently taken either it or a chemically similar drug;

g some people develop a hypersensitivity to the drug as a result of having previously taken a dose of it.

The patient's reaction will also depend upon the regularity with which he takes a drug he has been prescribed. Left to administer it to himself, he may forget to take a dose or deliberately not take it while declaring that he has. People most likely to cheat are:

● patients who have experienced adverse reactions to the drug;

● patients who have to take several drugs or are on a complex regime of drugs;

● socially isolated people.

Drug interactions

More than one drug may be administered to a patient at the same time. Special care has to be taken when a patient is receiving more than one drug for they may react with one another and cause undesirable effects. Drug interaction is not, however, always harmful and some of it may benefit a patient.

Drug interaction may:

a increase the effect of one or more of the drugs;
b reduce the effect of one or more of the drugs;
c produce other reactions.

The drugs most likely to cause harmful reactions are:

anticoagulant drugs	antidiabetic drugs
digoxin	cytotoxic drugs
monoamine oxidase inhibitor tranquillisers	

Any patient receiving one of these drugs is at risk should he take another.

Less dangerous drugs are:

antidepressants	anticonvulsants
antihypertensive drugs	
drugs given for angina pectoris	

Interaction of drugs with alcohol and food

Some drugs can cause dangerous reactions when a patient who is taking them also takes alcohol or some foods.
Warfarin reacts with alcohol to cause haemorrhages.
Insulin reacts with alcohol to cause hypoglycaemia.
Monoamine oxidase inhibitor tranquillisers react with tyramine, a substance present in cheese, yoghurt, broad beans, meat extract and red wine, to cause hypertensive crises.

If a nurse is worried about a drug, its dose, or any reactions she thinks it may have produced, she should consult the doctor who prescribed it or the hospital pharmacist.

Drugs in Pregnancy and Labour

Drugs taken by a pregnant woman should be limited to those that are absolutely necessary and those that are taken should be taken in the smallest effective dose. New drugs are regarded with suspicion. This is because some drugs taken by a pregnant woman can harm the fetus.

(a) First three months

During the first three months after conception the tissues and organs are being organized into their final or near final form. Some drugs taken by the mother during this period may cause either the death and abortion of the fetus or congenital abnormalities. Cytotoxic drugs (see Section 36) are known to do this because they interfere with cell division. Drugs suspected of doing it include anti-convulsants, antihistamines, anti-emetics and tranquillisers.

(b) Fourth to Ninth Month

During this stage of pregnancy many drugs taken by the mother are capable of passing through the placenta into the baby. This is called crossing the placental barrier. When it happens, the concentration of the drug in the baby's blood plasma becomes as high as the concentration of it in the mother's blood plasma. Some drugs can harm the baby, e.g.:

  i   tetracyclines affect the growth of the baby's bones and teeth,

  ii corticosteroids affect the baby's growth,

  iii streptomycin can make him deaf by damaging the auditory nerve,

  iv antithyroid drugs can produce a fetal goitre,

  v drugs of addiction can produce a drug-addicted baby.

(c) Labour

Drugs given to a mother during or just before labour can harm the baby, e.g.

  i   general anaesthetics can depress the baby's respiration,
  ii anticoagulants (see Section 4) can cause haemorrhages,
 iii sulphonamides (see Section 1) can cause severe and sometimes fatal jaundice.

Infant feeding

Some of any drug taken by a mother is likely to appear in breast milk. A mother who has to take drugs regularly (e.g. for epilepsy) should not breast-feed.

Drugs in Old age

In old age drugs should be given in small doses and their effects reviewed every 2–3 days at first. Liver and kidney functions may be impaired by degeneration, and this can effect the breakdown and excretion of drugs. Complicated drug routines are to be avoided, and if an old person is muddled and forgetful someone else should look after and give the drugs.

1 · Antibacterial Drugs

Antibacterial drugs are used to treat infections by bacteria. Some of these drugs are antibiotics, i.e. they are obtained from living organisms; others, such as the sulphonamides, are chemically manufactured substances.

These drugs attack bacteria, but in the doses normally given do not attack the cells of the body. They appear to act in three different ways:

a the penicillins and some other antibiotics destroy the cell-wall of bacteria and so kill them;

b the tetracyclines, streptomycin and some other antibiotics attack the cell nucleus of bacteria and so prevent them from multiplying;

c the sulphonamides interfere with the metabolism of bacteria and prevent them from having harmful effects.

Many of these drugs are effective against many kinds of bacteria. They should not be used indiscriminately to treat minor infections from which the patient is likely to recover without special treatment. One of the dangers in their use is the development of a strain of bacteria which is resistant to the drug. A resistant strain is one against which a particular drug has no effect. Some of these resistant strains are probably those which were originally immune to action by the drug and have been able to multiply when other, non-resistant strains were being killed; but resistance can develop if the drug is given in too small doses for too short a time, and if an antibacterial drug is given, it should be given in adequate doses for at least five days.

In the choice of a particular drug several factors have to be considered:

a if there is time the 'sensitivity' of the bacteria to several drugs is tested in the laboratory, and the choice made of that drug which most quickly kills the bacteria;

b in some infections a particular drug is known to be the most effective, e.g. chloramphenicol in the treatment of typhoid fever;

c drugs which are not readily absorbed by the intestine are used to treat intestinal infections;

d drugs which are excreted by the kidneys in an active
form are used to treat urinary infections;

e special care has to be taken with some drugs (e.g.
penicillin) which can produce hypersensitivity reactions
when a patient has become hypersensitive to them by
having taken the drug previously.

If a patient is acutely ill or laboratory facilities are not
available, choice has to be made of the drug most likely
to be effective or one which is known to kill a wide range
of bacteria.

Benzylpenicillin

Other names. Penicillin, penicillin G, crystalline penicillin
G.

Proprietary name. Crystapen G.

Dose. For an adult: 125–500 mg every 4 hours by mouth;
or 150–600 mg 2–12 times daily by intramuscular
injection.

For a child under 1 year: 62.5 mg (100 000 units),
every 6 hours by mouth or intramuscular injection.

For a child 1–5 years: 150 mg (250 000 units), every
6 hours by mouth or intramuscular injection.

For a child 6–12 years: 250 mg (400 000 units), every
6 hours by mouth or intramuscular injection.

Actions and uses. Benzylpenicillin (the original penicillin G)
is an antibiotic which is active against a large number
of organisms. It is effective in haemolytic streptococcal
infections (e.g. acute throat infections, puerperal fever,
wound sepsis); in pneumonia; in gonorrhoea and
syphilis; in streptococcal, staphylococcal and pneu-
monococcal meningitis; in anthrax.

In spite of the discovery of many other antibiotics,
benzylpenicillin is still the best for many infections. It
is not active against staphylococci that produce penicillinase, an enzyme that destroys penicillin. Resistant
strains of any organisms can develop – especially of
staphylococci – and against them penicillin is useless.

Benzylpenicillin is usually given by intramuscular
injection. As it diffuses rapidly through the tissues and
is rapidly excreted, it has to be given at intervals of

not more than 6 hours. Slowly-acting penicillins are available. Benzylpenicillin appears in the cerebrospinal fluid only if the meninges are inflamed and high doses are given.

Toxic and side effects. The drug is relatively non-toxic, but in persons sensitive to it allergic reactions, sometimes of some severity, can occur; skin rashes, enlarged joints, and even anaphylactic shock and death. The drug is contraindicated in any person who has ever shown an acute reaction to it.

Benethamine Penicillin

Proprietary name. Triplopen.

Dose. 300–600 mg by intramuscular injection.

Actions and uses. Triplopen is a combination of benethamine penicillin, procaine penicillin and sodium penicillin. Benethamine and procaine penicillin are slow acting, and as they are not immediately effective, sodium penicillin is included to provide immediate cover. A single dose of the combined penicillin, injected intramuscularly, remains effective for 3–4 days.

Toxic and side effects. Similar to those of benzylpenicillin.

Benzathine Penicillin

Other names. Benzathine penicillin G, dibenzylamine penicillin G.

Proprietary name. Penidural.

Dose. For an adult: 900 mg by intramuscular injection every 2–3 weeks.

Actions and uses. This variety of penicillin is very slowly absorbed after intramuscular injection. The effects of one injection can persist for over a week. Repeated injections are therefore avoided. It is used prophylactically to prevent attacks of rheumatic fever, after tonsillectomy and after dental extractions. When used to treat acute infections, an initial dose of benzylpenicillin is given to provide penicillin cover until the slowly-acting drug starts to work.

Toxic and side effects. Similar to those of benzylpenicillin. Pain and tenderness can occur at the site of injection.

Phenoxy-methyl-penicillin

Other name. Penicillin V.

Proprietary names. Crystapen V, Distaquaine V, Icipen V, Penavlon V.

Dose. For an adult: 125–250 mg every 4 hours. For a child: 60–125 mg every 4 hours. For an infant: 30–60 mg every 4 hours.

Actions and uses. This is a form of penicillin that is absorbed from the gastrointestinal tract and can therefore be given by mouth. It is given as a tablet or capsule, preferably about half an hour before meals. The intervals between doses should not be more than 4 hours. For severe infections the dose is increased and the interval between doses reduced.

Toxic and side effects. It can produce diarrhoea. It is contra-indicated in patients who are sensitive to penicillin or have an allergy such as asthma.

Ampicillin

Proprietary name. Penbritin.

Dose. 250–500 mg every 6 hours.

Actions and uses. It is an antibiotic which is active against a large number of organisms, and is used for infections of the respiratory tract, the urinary tract and the gastro-intestinal tract. It has been recommended for the treatment of typhoid carriers. Doses of 1 g are given for gonorrhoea when resistance to penicillin has developed.

Toxic and side effects. Toxic effects are slight. Some patients may develop a slight rash; babies may develop loose stools.

Cloxacillin

Proprietary name. Orbenin.

Dose. 500 mg every 6 hours by mouth; or 250 mg every 4 hours by intramuscular injection.

Actions and uses. It is an antibiotic that is resistant to penicillinase, the enzyme that prevents other antibiotics from acting on staphylococci. It is used mainly in the treatment of staphylococcal infections that have proved to be resistant to other antibiotics.

Erythromycin

Proprietary names. Erythrocin, Ilotycin.

Dose. For an adult: 1–2 g daily in divided doses. For a child: 30 mg per kilo of body-weight daily every 6 hours.

Actions and uses. It is an antibiotic active against all the organisms that penicillin is active against. It is used mainly for those patients who are sensitive to penicillin. As gastric juice and the presence of food in the stomach cause it to decompose, it is administered in enteric-coated tablets, which dissolve only when they reach the small intestine.

Toxic and side effects. Nausea, vomiting and diarrhoea can occur.

Pivmecillinam

Proprietary name. Selexid.

Dose. 200 mg 4 times a day.

Actions and uses. It is an antibiotic used in urinary tract infections, Salmonella infections, septicaemia. It is not active against Gram-positive organisms.

Toxic and side effects. Loss of appetite, nausea, vomiting, indigestion: can be prevented by taking the drug with food.

Cefuroxine

Proprietary name. Zinacef.

Dose. 750 mg–1.5 g three times a day, by intramuscular or intravenous injection.

Actions and uses. This antibiotic is active against many organisms and has been used in the treatment of respiratory infections, penicillin-resistant gonorrhoea, etc.

Toxic and side effects. Thrombophlebitis; pain at site of injection.

Cefoxitin

Proprietary name. Mefoxin.

Dose. 1–2 g every 8 hours.

Actions and uses. This is an antibiotic active against many organisms and has been used in the treatment of abdominal sepsis, obstetric and gynaecological infections, gonorrhoea, etc.

Toxic and side effects. Thrombophlebitis; pain at site of injection.

Cefamandole

Proprietary name. Kefadol.

Dose. 500 mg–2 g every 4–8 hours.

Actions and uses. This antibiotic is active against many organisms and has been used in the treatment of respiratory infections, influenzal meningitis, etc.

Toxic and side effects. Thrombophlebitis; pain at injection site.

Tetracycline Hydrochloride

Proprietary names. Achromycin, Ambramycin, Economycin, Tetracyn, Totomycin.

Dose. For an adult: 250 mg every 6 hours. For a child: 10–30 mg per kilo of body-weight daily in divided doses.

Actions and uses. This is one of the tetracycline antibiotics, which have most actions in common. It is effective against very many organisms, but it is of particular value only in typhoid fever, paratyphoid fever, and rickettsial infections. It can be useful in the treatment of 'mixed' infections, as can occur in septic abortion and in peritonitis due to a gastric or intestinal perforation, but it is then usually given with another drug such as a sulphonamide.

The usefulness of tetracycline and other drugs of the same group is limited by the frequent development and persistence of resistant strains of the infecting organisms. This resistance has developed extensively since the drugs were first used. Cross-resistance develops (i.e. an organism that becomes resistant to one tetracycline becomes resistant to all drugs of the same group).

Other conditions that are sometimes still treated by tetracycline are staphylococcal and streptococcal infections, amoebic dysentery, and infections of the urinary tract; but for these infections other drugs (e.g. erythromycin, novobiocin, phenoxymethyl penicillin for staphylococcal infections) are now available that are less liable to encounter resistance and less liable to produce side-effects by disturbing the normal flora of the intestine. Tetracycline can be used prophylactically for chronic bronchitis, but resistant organisms are likely to develop before long. The drug has no effect on true virus infections (e.g. smallpox, influenza, poliomyelitis).

If the drug is administered by mouth for more than a week, vitamins of the B group should be given.

Toxic and side effects. Gastrointestinal disturbances occur; to prevent them the drug should be taken just after a meal, but not with milk (which prevents its absorption). Allergic skin rashes and fever can occur. Prolonged treatment may cause a deficiency of vitamin B group or irritation of the anal region by the development of fungi. The drug is deposited in the teeth of newly born babies, and when they appear they may be stained yellow; to prevent damage to bones and teeth, tetracyclines should not be used for long periods after the fourth month of pregnancy or given to children under 7 years. It is used with caution in any patient with kidney or liver disease, especially during pregnancy.

Staphylococcal entero-colitis is a severe and sometimes fatal complication due to the development of resistant staphylococci in the bowel. If it occurs the drug must be stopped at once.

Doxycycline Hydrochloride

Proprietary name. Vibramycin.

Dose. 200 mg on 1st day, followed by 100 mg daily in the morning.

Actions and uses. It actions and uses are similar to those of tetracycline hydrochloride, but it has the advantage that only one daily dose is required.

Toxic and side effects. Similar to those of tetracycline hydrochloride.

Minocycline Hydrochloride

Proprietary name. Minocin.

Dose. 200 mg on 1st day, followed by 100 mg twice daily.

Actions and side effects. Similar to those of tetracycline hydrochloride.

Toxic and side effects. Similar to those of tetracycline hydrochloride.

Chlortetracycline Hydrochloride

Proprietary name. Aureomycin.

Dose. 250 mg every 6 hours.

Actions and uses. This is a tetracycline antibiotic, with actions and uses similar to those of tetracycline itself.

Toxic and side effects. Similar to those of tetracycline. It is deposited in growing bones and may cause some damage to them.

Oxytetracycline

Proprietary names. Imperacin, Oxymycin, Terramycin.

Dose. For an adult: 250 mg every 6 hours by mouth; or 1–2 g by intravenous injection.
For a child: 10–30 mg per kilo of body-weight daily in divided doses, by mouth; or 10–20 mg per kilo of body-weight daily in divided doses by intravenous injection.

Actions and uses. Similar to those of tetracycline. It can be given as an ointment for staphylococcal infections of the skin, and as a 0.5 per cent ointment or drops for infections of the eye.

Toxic and side effects. Similar to those of tetracycline.

Methacycline

Proprietary name. Rondomycin.

Dose. Adult: 300–600 mg daily in divided doses.
Child: 3–6 mg/lb body-weight daily.

Actions and uses. It is an antibiotic, used particularly in the treatment of infections of the lungs and of the upper respiratory tract. It is valuable in the treatment of acute and chronic bronchitis. It is more effective than tetracycline.

Toxic and side effects. Gastrointestinal upsets can occur, but are usually mild and not an indication to stop the drug.

Bacitracin

Dose. As an intestinal antiseptic: 200 000 units every 4 hours by mouth.

Actions and uses. It is an antibiotic effective against a large number of organisms. Bacitracin is used: (a) in intestinal infections; (b) as a lotion, spray or ointment in the treatment of impetigo, sycosis barbae, other superficial infections of the skin, burns and wounds.

Toxic and side effects. When it is given by mouth so little is absorbed that toxic effects are not to be expected.

Chloramphenicol

Proprietary name. Chloromycetin.

Dose. For an adult: 1.5–3 g daily in divided doses.
   For a child: 25–50 mg per kilo of body-weight daily in divided doses.

Actions and uses. It is an antibiotic effective against a large number of organisms. Because of its serious toxic effects, its use is limited to the treatment of: (a) typhoid and paratyphoid fever, (b) rickettsial infections which have not responded to tetracyclines, (c) chronic urinary tract infections by *Proteus vulgaris* which have not responded to other drugs, (d) in meningitis due to *H. influenzae.*
   It can be used as a local application for infections of the eye and skin.

Toxic and side effects. Mild toxic effects are dryness of the mouth and gastrointestinal upsets. Thrush and other fungal infections may develop in the mucous membranes of the mouth, gastrointestinal tract and vagina (because of its effects on the normal bacteria present there). Most serious of its toxic effects – those that limit its use – are those on the bone-marrow. It can cause aplastic anaemia, agranulocytosis and purpura. Aplastic anaemia has occurred several months after the cessation of treatment. It should not be given to premature babies.

Cephaloridine

Proprietary name. Ceporin

Dose. Up to 5 g daily in divided doses by intramuscular injection.

Actions and uses. It is a semi-synthetic antibiotic which is effective against a wide range of organisms. It is used in the treatment of respiratory tract infections, urinary tract infections, meningitis, otitis media, endocarditis and staphylococcal infections which have become resistant to penicillin. It does not affect the organisms normally present in the bowel. Intramuscular injection should be painless; cephaloridine can be given intravenously or intrathecally in emergencies.

Cephalexin (proprietary names Ceporex, Keflex) is an oral preparation given in doses of up to 4 g daily in divided doses.

Toxic and side effects. Skin rashes may occur. Renal function is rarely disturbed.

Kanamycin Sulphate

Proprietary names. Kannasyn, Kantrex.

Dose. For an adult: 1–2 g daily in divided doses.

Actions and uses. It is an antibiotic used in the treatment of staphylococcal infections, respiratory infections and urinary tract infections.

Toxic and side effects. It is contra-indicated when renal function is impaired. Tinnitus and deafness can be produced if the drug is administered for more than 10 days, and it is advisable that it should not be continued for more than a week.

Neomycin Sulphate

Proprietary names. Mycifradin, Nivemycin.

Dose. For general infections: 500 mg–1 g daily in divided doses by intramuscular injection.

As an intestinal antiseptic: 2–8 g daily in divided doses by mouth.

Actions and uses. It is an antibiotic effective against a large number of organisms. Little of the drug is absorbed from the gastrointestinal tract when it is given by mouth, and it is used in the treatment of infections of the gastrointestinal tract and before operations upon it. Because of its toxic effects, its use is otherwise limited to the treatment of infections that have not responded to sulphonamides or other antibiotics.

It is used as a spray, lotion or ointment for the treatment of infections of the skin, and in eye-drops for conjunctivitis and blepharitis. In these preparations it is often combined with hydrocortisone, which reduces inflammation.

Toxic and side effects. Two serious side effects limit its use by intramuscular injection: (a) it has toxic effects on the kidneys and should not be used if renal function is at all impaired; and (b) it has toxic effects on the eighth (auditory) cranial nerve and can produce incurable deafness; it is contra-indicated for any person who is partially deaf.

Novobiocin

Other names. Novobiocin calcium, novobiocin sodium.

Proprietary name. Albamycin T (with tetracycline).

Dose. For an adult: 1–2 g daily in divided doses by mouth; or 500 mg by very slow intravenous injection.

For a child: 20–45 mg per kilo of body-weight in divided doses by mouth; or 15 mg per kilo of body-weight every 12 hours by very slow intravenous injection.

Actions and uses. This antibiotic (which is available as a calcium salt and a sodium salt) is used in the treatment of staphylococcal infections. It is usually given by mouth, but it can be given by intravenous injection. Intramuscular injection is painful and is not used. Toxic effects are common and resistant strains can develop. It is used mainly when other antibodies have failed.

Toxic and side effects. Toxic effects are common. They include pyrexia, skin rashes, nausea and vomiting. Leucopenia (a reduction in the number of white cells) is a more serious effect, and is especially liable to occur if the administration of the drug is continued for a long time. The skin can go yellow, but this is not important.

Colomycin

Other names. Colistin sulphate, colistin methane-sulphonate.

Proprietary name. Colomycin.

Dose. Colistin sulphate: 100 000–150 000 units per kilo of
body-weight daily in divided doses every 8 hours by
mouth.

    Colistin methane-sulphonate: 50 000–100 000 units per
kilo of body-weight daily in divided doses by intramuscular injection.

Actions and uses. It is an antibiotic available in two forms:
colimycin sulphate and colimycin methanesulphonate.
Colimycin sulphate is given by mouth, mainly in the
treatment of intestinal infections in children. Colimycin
methane-sulphonate is given by intramuscular injection
for many forms of infection; e.g. meningitis, septicaemia, urinary tract infections.

    Local applications of colimycin can be used to treat
infected skins or to prevent the infection of burns and
scalds.

Polymyxin B Sulphate

Proprietary name. Aerosporin.

Dose. By mouth: 1–2 million units every 4 hours.

By intramuscular injection: 500 000 units every 8 hours.

For a child: up to 40 000 units per kilo/weight, three times a day.

Actions and uses. It is an antibiotic active against a number of organisms, e.g. *E. coli*, *H. influenzae*, *B. pertussis*. It is especially useful in infections caused by *Pseudomonas pyocyanea*. It is used in the treatment of general and urinary tract infections. It may be given by mouth in the treatment of dysentery, or by intramuscular injection in the treatment of other infections. For urinary infections the dose can be reduced because the drug is excreted by the kidneys. But its toxic effects on the nervous system limit its use.

It can be applied as a lotion, spray or ointment to the skin in the treatment of scalds, burns and staphylococcal infections.

Toxic and side effects. Given by injection it can cause dizziness, and sensory disturbances in the face, arms and legs, but the occurrence of these is not an indication for stopping treatment.

It should not be given to patients with any degree of renal impairment, because it can have toxic effects on the renal tubules.

Gentamicin Sulphate

Proprietary names. Cidomycin, Garamycin, Genticin.

Dose. 60 kilo and over, 80 mg 8 hourly intramuscularly or intravenously; under 60 kilo, 60 mg 8 hourly.

Actions and uses. It is an antibiotic used in life-threatening infections and infections caused by resistant organisms. It can be given as a cream or ointment. It is applied locally as a 0.1–0.3 per cent cream or ointment.

Toxic and side effects. It can produce deafness and dizziness by damaging the inner ear, and as it can impair kidney function it is not given to patients with kidney disease.

Lincomycin Hydrochloride

Proprietary names. Lincocin, Mycivin.

Dose. By mouth: Adults and children over 10: 500 mg three or four times daily.
Children under 10: 30–60 mg per kilo of body-weight per day, divided into 3–4 equal doses.
By intramuscular injection:
Adults and children over 10: 600 mg every 12–24 hours.
Children under 10: 10 mg per kilo of body-weight every 12–24 hours.

Actions and uses. It is an antibiotic used in the treatment of pneumonia, streptococcal infections of nose, throat and ear, osteomyelitis and staphylococcal infections of the skin. For severe infections it is given intravenously in glucose saline.

Toxic and side effects. Loose stools may appear. No serious hypersensitivity reactions have been reported, but nausea, abdominal pains, itching and rashes have occurred.

Clindamycin

Proprietary name. Dalacin C.

Dose. Adults: 150–450 mg every 6 hours.
   Children: 16–20 mg per kilo body-weight daily in divided doses.

Actions and uses. It is an antibiotic used in the treatment of osteomyelitis, septic arthritis, respiratory tract and ENT infections, soft tissue and skin infection and dental and blood infections. It does not penetrate the blood-brain barrier in the therapeutically effective amounts.

Toxic and side effects. Abdominal discomfort, diarrhoea, nausea, occasionally vomiting and rarely rashes can occur. Colitis can occur, and this is an indication for stopping the drug.

Talampicillin Hydrochloride

Proprietary name. Talpen.

Dose. 250 mg three times daily.

Actions and uses. It is an oral antibiotic used in the treatment of many infections, especially bronchitis, pneumonia, infections of ear, nose and throat, urinary tract infections, gynaecological infections, and skin and soft tissue infections. For the treatment of gonorrhoea it is given in a single dose of 1.5–2.0 g.

Toxic and side effects. An erythematous rash and diarrhoea can occur. It is not recommended for patients with severe impairment of kidney or liver function, and is not given to patients with penicillin hypersensitivity.

Co-trimoxazole

Proprietary names. Septrin, Bactrim (Trimethoprim with Sulphamethoxazole).

Dose. Adults and children over 12 years: 2 tablets of Septrin twice daily.
Children 6–12 years: 1 tablet twice daily.

Actions and uses. This combination is a synthetic anti-bacterial substance which kills bacteria and inhibits bacterial growth. It is used to treat bacterial infection, especially infection of the lung and the urinary tract. In acute infection treatment is continued for at least 5 days or until symptoms have been absent for 24–48 hours. Because of its toxicity it is not used for minor infections, e.g. tonsillitis.

Toxic and side effects. Headache, nausea, vomiting and rashes can occur. Blood-formation may be disturbed by prolonged administration.

Sodium Fusidate

Proprietary name. Fucidin.

Dose. 250 mg three times a day.

Actions and uses. It is a 'steroid antibiotic' effective against organisms of various kinds (but particularly staphylococci which are resistant to penicillin) even when they are enclosed within fibrous tissue, inflamed bone, or the crusts on burns. It is used to treat staphylococcal infections of bone, skin, meninges, bowel, heart, etc.

Toxic and side effects. There are no known contra-indications. Although similar in composition to hormonal steroids, it has no hormonal effects. Nausea and vomiting are avoided by giving it with food.

Nalidixic Acid

Proprietary names. Negram, Neggram, Wynto-mylon.

Dose. Adults: 1 g four times a day for 7 days.
   Children: 60 mg per kilo bodyweight per day.

Actions and uses. It is an anti-bacterial agent used in the treatment of acute and chronic urinary-tract infections due to Gram-negative organisms, especially *E. coli* and *B. proteus*.

Toxic and side effects. It is used cautiously when there is any respiratory depression. Side effects are mild: they include gastrointestinal disturbance, dizziness, itching, urticaria and visual disturbance. Exposure to sunlight should be avoided as photo-sensitivity reactions of the skin can occur; if they do, the drug is stopped. Overdosage is treated by stomach wash-outs and respiratory stimulation.

Nitrofurantoin

Proprietary names. Furadantin, N-Fur.

Dose. 50–100 mg 4 times a day.

Actions and uses. It is an antibacterial drug, chiefly used for bacterial infections of the urinary tract. It should be given during or immediately after meals. Treatment should not be continued for more than 14 days. At least 4 weeks should elapse between courses of treatment.

Toxic and side effects. Nausea and vomiting can occur. Peripheral neuritis can be caused. It is contra-indicated for patients with severe kidney disease.

Amoxycillin

Proprietary name. Amoxil.

Dose. 250–500 mg 3 times a day.
   Children up to 10 years: 125 mg 3 times a day. In severe infections twice the dose can be given.

Actions and uses. It is a semi-synthetic penicillin used in the treatment of chest infections, urinary infections, gonorrhoea, etc.

Toxic and side effects. It should not be given to patients who are hypersensitive to penicillin.

Cefaclor

Proprietary name. Distaclor

Dose. 250 mg 8-hourly.

Actions and uses. It is antibacterial drug given by mouth and most effective against mild or moderate infections by staphylococci, streptococci and other organisms.

Toxic and side effects. Diarrhoea. Vaginal candidiasis.

Sulphadimidine

Proprietary name. Sulphamezathine.

Dose. In urinary infections: 2 g followed by up to 4 g daily in divided doses.

In general infections: 3 g followed by up to 6 g daily in divided doses.

By intramuscular or intravenous injection: 1–2 g.

Actions and uses. The actions of this drug are typical of many sulphonamides, but as it is readily absorbed and less toxic than the others it is the drug of choice for infections other than those of the bowel. It is used in the treatment of meningococcal meningitis, pneumococcal meningitis, pneumococcal pneumonia, streptococcal infections, and *E. coli* infections of the urinary tract. Like other sulphonamides it is less effective in staphylococcal infections. It can be given by intramuscular or intravenous injection when rapid action is required, but it must not be given by intrathecal injection (i.e. by lumbar or cisternal puncture).

Toxic and side effects. Toxic and side effects are rare. Some patients are hypersensitive to any sulphonamide and show it by developing nausea, vomiting, skin rashes and pyrexia. Sulphonamides are contra-indicated in patients with hypersensitivity, renal disease, jaundice and liver dysfunction.

Sulphafurazole

Proprietary name. Gantrisin.

Dose. Initial dose 2 to 4 g, then 1–2 g every 4–6 hours.

Actions and uses. This sulphonamide is commonly used for urinary tract infections. It can be used for other infections.

Toxic and side effects. Similar to those of sulphadimidine.

Sulphamethizole

Proprietary name. Urolucosil.

Dose. 100–200 mg.

Actions and uses. This sulphonamide is effective in small doses in urinary tract infections. It is the only sulphonamide for which fluid intake should be decreased (except in hot climates), in order to increase the concentration of it in the urine.

Toxic and side effects. Rare.

Sulphasalazine

Proprietary name. Salazopyrin.

Dose. 1.0–2.0 g every 6 hours.

Actions and uses. It is used in the treatment of acute attacks of ulcerative colitis and regional enteritis. Larger doses of the drug, if the patient can tolerate them, may be used.

Toxic and side effects. Nausea, vomiting, headache and malaise can be produced by large doses. Allergic rashes and fever occur sometimes. More serious effects are a reduction in the number of white cells in the blood and a form of haemolytic anaemia.

Sulfametopyrazine

Proprietary name. Kelfizine W.

Dose. 2 g once weekly.

Actions and uses. It is used for renal infections, upper and lower respiratory tract infections, and other infections.

Toxic and side effects. As for other sulpha drugs. It is given cautiously when renal function is impaired.

Sulphamethoxypyridazine

Proprietary name. Lederkyn.

Dose. For severe infections: 2 g followed by 1 g every
24 hours.
    For mild infections: 1 g followed by 500 mg every
24 hours.

Actions and uses. This is a long-acting sulphonamide of
which only one dose need be given in every 24 hours.
It can be used in the treatment of the infections that
respond to sulphonamide therapy, but it is not very
effective in urinary infections because the concentration
in the urine is low. Its toxic effects limit its use.

Toxic and side effects. Toxic effects are common. Mild
toxic effects include pyrexia, nausea, headache, giddiness, painful joints and skin rashes. Among the more
serious side effects are purpura, aplastic anaemia,
leucopenia, hepatitis and myocarditis. These can be
severe, and death has occurred after it use.

Sulphamethoxydiazine

Proprietary name. Durenate.

Dose. 1 g on 1st day, followed by 500 mg on subsequent
days.

Actions and uses. It is a sulpha drug used in the treatment
of upper respiratory tract infections, otitis media,
tonsillitis and other infections.

Toxic and side effects. It is contra-indicated when a patient
is known to be sensitive to sulphonamides or has
impaired renal function. It should not be given to
infants under 3 months old or to pregnant women in
the week of expected delivery.

Phthalylsulphathiazole

Proprietary names. Sulphaphalidine, Thalazole.

Dose. 5–10 g daily in divided doses.

Actions and uses. Only slight amounts of this sulphonamide are absorbed from the gastrointestinal tract. It is used before and after operations on the large intestine in order to prevent the development of peritonitis or abscesses; it is used in the treatment of bacillary dysentery and ulcerative colitis.

Toxic and side effects. So little is absorbed that toxic effects are not to be expected. But if its use is continued for a long time, an overgrowth of moulds (of the *Candida* variety) can occur because the bacilli that normally keep them in check cease to exist in the bowel; this growth can cause a troublesome looseness of the bowels.

Succinylsulphathiazole

Proprietary names. Cremosuxidine, Sulfasuxidine.

Dose. 10–20 g daily in divided doses.

Actions and uses. Similar to phthalylsulphathiazole. It is not as effective.

Toxic and side effects. Similar to phthalylsulphathiazole.

2 · Drugs for Tuberculosis

The usual methods of treating tuberculosis are:
(a) a long-term method using three drugs – streptomycin, isoniazid and sodium aminosalicylate (PAS);
(b) a short-term method based on rifampicin.

In both methods one drug is not used alone because of the ability of the micro-organism to develop resistance to it. Resistance to a drug rarely develops when two are given together.

In the *long-term method* streptomycin, isoniazid and PAS are given for the first 2–3 months. A common way is to give isoniazid 300 mg with PAS 12 g daily by mouth in two divided doses and an intramuscular injection of streptomycin 1 g daily for patients under 40 years of age and 750 mg daily for patients over 40. Then, for the next 18–24 months two drugs are given, usually isoniazid and PAS. If this treatment is carried out in full, almost all cases will be cured; but it is sometimes difficult to persuade patients to continue to take tablets or big cachets when they are feeling well, and many default.

In the *short-term method* (a) rifampicin and isoniazid are given with either ethambutol or streptomycin for the first 8 weeks, and then (b) rifampicin with isoniazid for 7 months.

Cycloserine, ethionamide, thiacetazone and pyrazinamide are other drugs sometimes used in the treatment of tuberculosis.

Streptomycin Sulphate

Dose. 750 mg–1 g once daily by intramuscular injection.

Actions and uses. Streptomycin is an antibiotic used to treat all forms of tuberculosis. Resistance to the drug may develop rapidly and last for life. The drug is always given with isoniazid or PAS, as it is unlikely that the same organisms would be resistant to more than one drug.

Streptomycin is excreted unchanged and still active in the urine. It is sometimes used for the treatment of *B. proteus* infections of the urinary tract. Because of the danger of resistance developing it is not used for other infections. Smaller doses than usual are given to old patients and to patients with impaired renal function.

Toxic and side effects. Mild toxic effects are nausea, fever and a rash. A serious toxic effect is a permanent disturbance of the inner ear. The patient develops giddiness and deafness, mostly high-tone. To some degree the giddiness remains permanent; and while the patient may learn to adjust to this in daylight, he is unsteady in the dark. Old people with impaired renal function are particularly liable to become deaf. Jaundice can occur.

Isoniazid

Proprietary names. Nicetal, Nydrazid, Pycazide.

Dose. 300–600 mg daily in divided doses.

Actions and uses. Isoniazid is a synthetic drug which acts by inhibiting the growth of *M. tuberculosis*; it can penetrate caseous lesions. It is always prescribed with another anti-tuberculosis drug. Tablets should not be left exposed to light.

Toxic and side effects. Neuropathy (prevented by pyridoxine 10 mg daily), confusion, jaundice and fits can occur with high doses.

Sodium Aminosalicylate

Other name. PAS (para-aminosalicyclic acid).

Proprietary names. Entepas, Paramisan, Pasade.

Dose. 10–15 g in divided doses.

Actions and uses. PAS is always given in combination with one or other of the other drugs. It has to be given in large doses, and having an unpleasant taste it is given in cachets. Patients usually dislike having to take such large doses and may secretly stop taking the cachets.

Toxic and side effects. It can cause some gastric upset, vomiting, fever, rashes and an enlarged spleen and lymph-nodes, and diarrhoea. Goitre and myxoedema can occur.

Thiacetazone

Dose. 150 mg daily.

Actions and uses. It is given in a single daily dose with isoniazid 300 mg. It is used as a substitute for PAS (a) for patients who cannot tolerate PAS, (b) in under-developed countries because it is cheaper than PAS.

Toxic and side effects. Allergic reactions can be severe.

Cycloserine

Proprietary name. Cycloserine.

Dose. 250–500 mg twice daily.

Actions and uses. It is an antibiotic which is effective against a large number of organisms. It is mainly used in the treatment of pulmonary tuberculosis. It is used when the patient is hypersensitive to streptomycin or the organism is resistant to it. It is given in combination with isoniazid or sodium aminosalicylate to reduce the possibility of a resistant strain developing.

It is also used for chronic urinary infections which are not responding to treatment by other drugs.

Toxic and side effects. Serious toxic effects can be produced, such as headache, dizziness, fits, confusion and depression. It is contra-indicated in epileptics and patients with a history of mental illness.

Ethionamide

Proprietary name. Trescatyl.

Dose. 500 mg twice daily.

Actions and uses. It is used in the treatment of pulmonary tuberculosis when the organism has become resistant to other drugs or the patient has become hypersensitive to them.

Toxic and side effects. It can cause nausea, jaundice and neuropathy.

Pyrazinamide

Proprietary name. Zinamide.

Dose. Up to 3 g daily in divided doses.

Actions and uses. It is an anti-tubercular drug, usually used in combination with another anti-tubercular drug. It is not considered to be a drug of first choice or one for use over a long period.

Toxic and side effects. As it has toxic effects on the liver, liver function tests should be done before this drug is used and fortnightly while it is being used. In people predisposed to gout, an attack of gout can be precipitated.

Ethambutol

Proprietary name. Myambutol

Dose. 25 mg per kilo of body-weight in single daily dose for 2 months, and then 15 mg per kilo.

Actions and uses. It is an anti-tubercular drug, used mainly for patients who cannot tolerate PAS. It is not effective when there are cavities in the lungs.

Toxic and side effects. Retrobulbar neuritis can occur. The patient's eyes should be examined before treatment and if any visual disturbance occurs.

Rifampicin

Proprietary names. Rifadin, Rimactane.

Dose. 10–20 mg per kilo body-weight in single daily dose, up to maximum of 600 mg.

Actions and uses. It is an anti-tubercular drug. It should be given on an empty stomach. Urine, sputum and tears may become brownish-red. Liver function tests are performed in early weeks of treatment.

Toxic and side effects. Gastrointestinal side effects and purpura can occur. It is given cautiously to patients whose liver-function may be impaired, e.g. alcoholics.

3 · Drugs Acting on the Heart

The drugs that act on the heart fall into the following groups:

a digitalis and its derivatives which act on conduction in the myocardium and are used for the treatment of congestive heart failure and certain disturbances of cardiac function;

b other drugs – such as aminophylline and quinidine – which also improve the efficiency of the myocardium;

c vaso-dilators used in the treatment of angina pectoris;

d anti-coagulants used in the treatment of coronary thrombosis and thrombosis in other vessels.

A number of drugs used in the treatment of angina pectoris and cardiac arrhythmias are called beta-blockers because they block the beta effects of adrenaline. By doing so they reduce the sympathetic pressure on the heart and reduce the work it has to do.

Other drugs which affect the function of the heart are anti-hypertensives, oxygen, and diuretics.

Digoxin

Proprietary name. Lanoxin.

Dose. Initial dose: 1–1.5 mg daily in a single dose or divided doses.

Maintenance dose: 250 mcg once or twice daily.

By intramuscular or slow intravenous injection: 750 mcg.

Actions and uses. Digoxin (which is obtained from the leaf of the woolly foxglove – *digitalis lanata*) is the best preparation of digitalis. The precise action of digitalis on the heart is not definitely known; but it affects failing heart muscle, causes more powerful contractions of the heart, and increases the output of blood with every contraction. The heart becomes smaller. Venous congestion is reduced; the output of urine is increased; oedema is reduced.

Digoxin is used for the prevention and treatment of congestive heart failure and for the control of atrial fibrillation. To produce rapid 'digitalization' (i.e. the control of the heart by digitalis), the relatively large dose of 1–1.5 mg is given once, by mouth; and when this shows effects, which it should do within 48–72 hours, the dose is reduced to a maintenance dose of 0.25 mg once to three times a day. The dose is adjusted to prevent too rapid a heart rate on exercise. Serum and plasma digoxin concentration can be accurately measured by radio-immunoassay. In emergencies an intramuscular or intravenous injection of the drug can be given; the patient must not have had digoxin or any similar drug by mouth for at least a fortnight previously.

Toxic and side effects. Toxic effects are particularly liable to occur in old people. Loss of appetite is the first sign that overdosage is beginning, and this is followed by nausea, vomiting and headache and diarrhoea. A dangerous depression of the heart's action can produce a very slow pulse; but paroxysmal tachycardia, coupling of the beats and extra-systoles can be other indications of over-digitalization. An excessive secretion of urine can cause a serious loss of potassium, which has to be replaced by potassium chloride or potassium citrate given by mouth. Facial neuralgia, visual disturbances, disorientation and other mental symptoms can occur. Toxic signs may persist for several days after the drug has been stopped.

Lanatoside C

Other name. Deslanoside.

Proprietary name. Cedilanid.

Dose. Initial dose: 1–1.5 mg.
    Subsequent doses: 250 mcg every 6 hours.

Actions and uses. Lanatoside C is a cardiac glycoside used to produce digitalization in the treatment of congestive heart failure and atrial fibrillation. In patients sensitive to digitalis it can produce digitalization without vomiting.

Toxic and side effects. Similar to those of digoxin.

Procainamide Hydrochloride

Proprietary name. Pronestyl.

Dose. By mouth: 250 mg every 4–6 hours.
    By slow intravenous injection: 100–1 000 mg.

Actions and uses. Its actions are similar to those of quinidine. It can be used to treat ventricular arrhythmias and extra-systoles. Administration by mouth is preferred.

Toxic and side effects. When the drug is given by mouth, vomiting can occur. Intravenous injection can cause a sharp drop in blood-pressure and collapse. Other indications for stopping the drug are anginal attacks and respiratory depression or over-stimulation. Pyrexia, rashes, enlarged lymph-nodes, joint swellings, eosinophilia and agranulocytosis can occur. Hallucinations and depression have been produced.

Nifedipine

Proprietary name. Adalat.

Dose. Starting dose: 10 mg 3 times a day.
   Increasing to: 20 mg 3 times a day.

Actions and uses. It is an anti-anginal drug which dilates
the coronary arteries. It is used to prevent angina of
effort, and for patients with angina at rest or due to
spasm of the coronary arteries.

Toxic and side effects. Flushing, dizziness, headaches, due
to vasodilatation.

Aminophylline

Proprietary names. Cardophylin, Diaphyllin.

Dose. 100–300 mg by mouth; 250–500 mg by very slow
intravenous injection; or 150–500 mg by suppository.

Actions and uses. Aminophylline is composed of theo-
phylline and ethylene-diamine (which makes the theo-
phylline soluble). Aminophylline stimulates the myocardium and increases the output of blood with each
contraction of the heart. It is particularly used for the
treatment of paroxysmal dyspnoea due to left ventricular
failure. When it is given by mouth its effects are
uncertain, and it is best given by injection or suppository.
   The same drug is used as a diuretic in the treatment
of oedema, and as a relaxant of involuntary muscle in
the prevention and treatment of asthma, bronchitis and
chest infections.

Toxic and side effects. When given by mouth it irritates
the stomach and can cause nausea and vomiting.

Glyceryl Trinitrate

Other name. Nitroglycerine.

Proprietary names. Nitrocine (capsule), Sustac.

Dose. 500 mcg–1 mg.

Actions and uses. It lowers venous and arterial vascular
resistance and reduces the demand for oxygen. It acts
within two minutes and its effects last for 30–40
minutes. Its chief value is to prevent attacks of angina,
the sensible patient taking one a few minutes before
he has to engage in work he knows is likely to bring
on an attack. The tablet should not be swallowed but
allowed to dissolve in the mouth, from the mucous
membrane of which it is readily absorbed.

Toxic and side effects. Some flushing of the face, pounding
of the heart, slight headache may occur at first, but
usually disappear with regular use of the drug.

Penta-Erythritol Tetranitrate

Proprietary names. Mycardol, Peritrate, Pentral 80 (slow
release).

Dose. 10–30 mg.

Actions and uses. The tablet (unlike a glyceryl trinitrate
tablet, which is allowed to dissolve in the mouth) is
swallowed. It is absorbed slowly and dilates blood-
vessels slowly. It begins to take effect in about 1 hour
and its effects last for about 5 hours. It is used to
prevent attacks of angina, and it is claimed that by taking it the patient does not need to take as many tablets
of glyceryl trinitrate.

Oxprenolol Hydrochloride

Proprietary name. Trasicor.

Dose. 40–160 mg 1–3 times daily.

Actions and uses. It is one of the beta-blocking drugs used in the treatment of cardiac arrhythmias and angina pectoris. When it is used for angina pectoris glyceryl trinitrate may not be necessary.

Toxic and side effects. Mild gastrointestinal disturbance, tiredness and dizziness can occur. If it causes slowing of the pulse or a fall in blood pressure, it is withdrawn and started later with a smaller dose.

Pindolol

Proprietary name. Visken.

Dose. 2.5–5.0 mg 3 times daily.

Actions and uses. It is a beta-blocking drug used in the treatment of angina pectoris.

Toxic and side effects. Depression, insomnia, headache, epigastric pain and diarrhoea can occur. It is used with caution in patients with a history of asthma or a recent myocardial infarction.

Timolol Maleate

Proprietary name. Blocadren.

Dose. 10–45 mg daily.

Actions and uses. It is a beta-blocking drug used for the treatment of angina pectoris due to ischaemic heart disease.

Toxic and side effects. Gastrointestinal symptoms and insomnia can occur. More serious side effects, for which the drug may have to be stopped, are marked slowing of the pulse and postural hypotension.

Sotalol Hydrochloride

Proprietary names. Beta-Cardone, Sotacar.

Dose. 120–240 mg daily in divided doses.

Actions and uses. It is a beta-blocking drug used for the treatment of cardiac arrhythmias and to reduce the frequency of attacks of angina pectoris, thereby lessening the need for glyceryl trinitrate.

Toxic and side effects. Some people have a hypersensitivity to the drug and can develop spasm of the bronchial muscle.

Bretylium Tosylate

Proprietary name. Bretylate.

Dose. 100 mcg per kilo body-weight by intramuscular injection; repeatable 6–8 hourly.

Actions and uses. It is an adrenergic-neurone blocking agent given in intensive care units when other treatments have failed to stop a ventricular dysrhythmia. It acts in 20–120 minutes.

Toxic and side effects. B.P. falls, and patient should be lying down during treatment. Vomiting is an indication to stop treatment or reduce dose. Noradrenaline should not be given at the same time. The drug should not be given intravenously.

Propranolol Hydrochloride

Proprietary name. Inderal.

Dose. 80–400 mg daily in divided doses.
  1–5 mg by intravenous injection.

Actions and uses. It is a beta-blocking drug which produces a slower and more effective heart-beat and lowers the blood-pressure. It has been used in the treatment of angina pectoris, paroxysmal tachycardia and high blood-pressure.

It is also used to prevent attacks of migraine as it may be able to prevent the painful dilatation of blood vessels which occurs in that condition.

Toxic and side effects. Side effects (such as tiredness, nausea, unsteadiness and giddiness) are usually slight and relieved by reducing the dose. It is contra-indicated in heart-failure and has to be used cautiously if the patient has a history of heart-failure. It is contra-indicated in patients with asthma and bronchospasm. Administration of it should stop 6 hours before ether or chloroform anaesthesia. Heart-block can be produced by intravenous injection; intravenous atropine 1.0–3.0 mg is the antidote. Sudden withdrawal or a big reduction in dose can cause myocardial infarction or an increase in angina pectoris.

Dopamine

Proprietary name. Intropin.

Dose. It is given by continuous intravenous infusion in a starting dose of 2 mcg per kilo of body weight per minute, increasing to about 10 mcg per kilo per minute.

Actions and uses. It is a naturally occurring substance and an intermediary in the formation of noradrenaline. It increases cardiac output and urine flow. It is used in the treatment of shock in myocardial infarction, trauma, septicaemia, renal failure, open-heart surgery and congestive heart failure. Treatment can be continued for hours or days; stopping it should be gradual.

Toxic and side effects. These are dose-dependent and include nausea, vomiting, headache, ectopic heart beats, rapid heart rate, angina pectoris, renal failure, hypertension. Necrosis of local tissue can occur if the drug leaks into the drip-site.

4 · Anti-coagulants

Anti-coagulants are drugs used to prevent the spread of an intravascular thrombosis and to reduce the risk of pulmonary embolism. They are used in the treatment of coronary thrombosis, deep venous thromboses in the legs, acute peripheral arterial blocking, thromboses in the retinal vessels, and embolism following atrial fibrillation.

Certain general principles are applicable to all anti-coagulants:

a The drugs should be used only in hospitals with laboratory facilities for estimating the clotting-time and prothrombin time.

b They are contra-indicated in renal disease, acute pulmonary tuberculosis, peptic ulcer, and hypo-pro-thrombinaemia.

c The dose should be reduced if salicylates are being given or if antibiotics are being given by mouth and so might prevent the formation of vitamin K in the bowel.

Any anti-coagulant can cause a haemorrhage. Although the risk is not great, massive bleeding into the brain or other organ can cause death. Haematuria and melaena are caused by minor bleeding into the urinary and gastro-intestinal tracts. Bleeding is most likely when:

a the patient has a disease of which bleeding is a feature,

b the patient is seriously ill and especially when he has disease of the liver,

c the patient is taking aspirin, salicylates or phenylbuta-zone,

d the patient stops taking phenobarbitone or glutethimide after having taken them for a long time.

Heparin

Other name. Heparin sodium.

Proprietary names. Pularin, Heparin Retard (a long-acting form of heparin given at intervals of 12 hours).

Dose. 30 000–40 000 units daily intravenously as 10 000 units 6-hourly, or 40 000 units given by continuous infusion with 500 ml Dextrose injection or Sodium Chloride injection. A high dose subcutaneous injection can be given.

Actions and uses. Heparin is an anti-coagulant (originally obtained from liver). It prevents the conversion of prothrombin to thrombin and the conversion of fibrinogen to fibrin, and so inhibits the clotting of blood. It is ineffective by mouth. It may have slight effects upon clots that have already formed; its main function is to prevent further clotting. While the treatment is being given no dose must be omitted, even at night.

Heparin is used in the treatment of coronary thrombosis and intravascular clotting elsewhere, and prophylactically in vascular surgery or to prevent thrombosis after any major surgical operation in which post-operative thrombosis is likely to occur. It can be given in combination with phenindione or other anti-coagulant given by mouth, the heparin being administered intravenously for the first 24-30 hours only while the oral anti-coagulant is becoming effective.

Toxic and side effects. Anaphylaxis can occur. Signs of over-dosage are bleeding from the gums or nose, the appearance of bruises and the appearance of red blood cells in the urine. More serious complications are haemothorax, haematuria, melaena, subarachnoid haemorrhage and retro-peritoneal haematoma. The patient should not also take aspirin as it could contribute to the bleeding by interfering with blood platelet function.

An over-dosage is treated by slow intravenous injection of protamine sulphate 50 mg.

Contra-indications are any known tendency to bleed, peptic ulcer, malignant disease, severe renal or hepatic disease, subacute bacterial endocarditis, and pregnancy. Menstruation (unless it is very excessive) is not a contra-indication.

Phenindione

Other name. Phenylindanedione.

Proprietary name. Dindevan.

Dose. Initial dose: 200–300 mg.
   Subsequent doses: 25–100 mg daily.

Actions and uses. Phenindione is an anti-coagulant which
acts by preventing the formation of 'factor VII' and
of prothrombin and so prolonging the prothrombin
time, which should be maintained at 2 to 2.5 times the
control time. It begins to be effective after about
24 hours, and heparin is usually given intravenously
to take effect until the phenindione can take over.
Subsequent doses are adjusted according to estimations
of the prothrombin time.

   It is used in the treatment of coronary thrombosis
and of thrombosis elsewhere (except in the cerebral
vessels). It does not affect any thrombus already
formed, but it prevents the spread of the thrombosis
and reduces the risk of embolism.

Toxic and side effects. It may produce a sore throat,
diarrhoea, skin rashes and pyrexia. Agranulocytosis is
a more serious effect. Bleeding from the gums, epistaxis
and the appearance of red blood cells in the urine are
signs of overdosage. Hepatic and renal damage can
occur. Acute ulcerative colitis has occurred. A redness
of the urine that the drug may produce is of no import-
ance.

   It is contra-indicated in cerebral thrombosis (because
of the danger of producing a cerebral haemorrhage),
when the patient has a tendency to bleed, in peptic
ulcer, malignant disease, renal or hepatic disease, and
pregnancy.

   Phytomenadione (Vitamin K_1; Proprietary name:
Konakion) is given in doses of 10–50 mg by mouth or
slow intravenous injection as an antidote to over-
dosage by phenindione.

Warfarin Sodium

Proprietary names. Marevan, Coumadin.

Dose. First dose: 30–50 mg.

Subsequent doses: 10–15 mg daily, according to patient's response.

Actions and uses. It is an anti-coagulant given by mouth or intravenous injection. The first dose must not exceed 50 mg. Plasma-concentrations and prothrombin times are estimated.

Warfarin is also used as a rat and squirrel poison.

Toxic and side effects. Haemorrhages and rashes can occur.

Phytomenadione (vitamin K₁) is an antidote for overdosage.

Ethyl Biscoumacetate

Proprietary name. Tromexan.

Dose. Initial dose: 1.2 g daily in divided doses.
Subsequent doses: 150–900 mg daily.

Actions and uses. Similar to those of phenindione.
Toxic and side effects. Similar to those of warfarin sodium.

Nicoumalone

Proprietary name. Sinthrome.

Dose. 1st day: 8–16 mg.
2nd day: 4–12 mg.
Maintenance dose according to clotting time.

Actions and uses. It is an anti-coagulant with a rapid action, a single dose producing the required effect in about 36 hours. It is not cumulative, and when treatment is stopped the prothrombin time becomes normal in about 24 hours.

Toxic and side effects. It is contra-indicated in bleeding diseases.

Phenprocoumon

Proprietary name. Liquamar.

Dose. Loading dose (first 36–48 hours): 27–39 mg.
   Maintenance dose: 750 mcg–6 mg.

Actions and uses. It is an anti-coagulant, acting slowly and taking 2–3 days to produce an effect.

Toxic and side effects. As it is cumulative the return of prothrombin-time to normal when treatment is stopped takes several days, and it is therefore difficult to check any bleeding that occurs. It is contra-indicated in severe kidney or liver disease, peptic ulcer, during pregnancy and after neurosurgery.

Streptokinase

Proprietary names. Kabikinase, Streptase.

Dose. Initial dose: 250 000–1 250 000 units.
   Maintenance dose: 100 000 units.

Actions and uses. It is a protein produced by some strains of streptococci and has the property of converting plasminogen into plasmin, an enzyme which can digest many proteins. As it digests clots and so opens up clotted blood-vessels, it is used in the treatment of severe thromboses – in deep vein thrombosis, pulmonary embolism, myocardial infarction, retinal artery and vein thrombosis.

Toxic and side effects. Immediate allergic reaction. Haemorrhage and Pyrexia.

Urokinase

Proprietary names. Ukidan, Urokinase Leo.

Dose. 5000–25 000 units.

Actions and uses. Similar to streptokinase.

Toxic and side effects. Similar to streptokinase.

5 · Vaso-constrictors

Vaso-constrictors are drugs used to raise the blood-pressure by their action in constricting the arterioles. They are used in the treatment of hypotension. Some act like nor-adrenaline on the nerve-endings of the sympathetic system, others act directly on the blood-vessels.

Nor-Adrenaline

Proprietary name. Levophed.

Dose. 0.5–2.5 ml per minute in intravenous saline transfusion of a solution of 8 micrograms per ml.

Actions and uses. This is the hormone produced at the nerve-endings of the post-ganglionic fibres of the sympathetic nervous system. It is given by slow intravenous infusion in the treatment of surgical shock. Treatment may have to be continued for many hours or several days.

It has an effect when applied to vessels directly, and a 1–5 000 solution can be applied to stop capillary bleeding, e.g. from the nose.

Toxic and side effects. Gangrene of the skin over the tip of the intravenous catheter can occur when treatment is continued for several hours, and if the skin there goes white or blue a new site for the infusion must be chosen. It is contra-indicated after myocardial infarction, if renal function is impaired, and during cyclopropane anaesthesia.

Methyl-Amphetamine

Dose. 10–30 mg by intravenous or intramuscular injection.

Actions and uses. It is dispensed in ampoules (30 mg in 1.5 ml). It is used in the treatment of hypotension caused by shock, vaso-vagal inhibition, surgical operations, injuries, and spinal anaesthesia. It is also used in the treatment of poisoning by barbiturates, morphine and other drugs.

    The drug is given by mouth (in doses of 2.5–10 mg daily) to treat obesity, alcoholism and parkinsonism.

Toxic and side effects. Anxiety, insomnia and restlessness can be produced.

Metaraminol Tartrate

Proprietary name. Aramine.

Dose. 500 mcg–5 mg intravenously in emergencies; 2–10 mg intramuscularly.

Actions and uses. It is a vaso-constrictor used in the treatment of hypotension during spinal anaesthesia.

Toxic and side effects. It is contra-indicated in cardiovascular disease, heart failure, hypertension, diabetes mellitus, and hyperthyroidism.

Mephentermine Sulphate

Proprietary name. Mephine.

Dose. First dose: 15 mg intravenously.
    Maintenance doses: 1–3 mg intramuscularly or intravenously.

Actions and uses. It is a vaso-constrictor used in the treatment of hypotension.

Toxic and side effects. It is contra-indicated when shock is secondary to haemorrhage.

Methoxamine Hydrochloride

Proprietary name. Vasoxine.

Dose. 10–15 mg by intramuscular injection; or 5–10 mg by intravenous injection.

Actions and uses. It constricts the blood-vessels and is injected intramuscularly or intravenously to raise or maintain the blood-pressure during an operation, especially when a spinal anaesthetic is being given.

It may be applied as a spray or as drops to relieve congestion of the mucous membrane of the nose in the common cold and most kinds of rhinitis.

Toxic and side effects. It produces vomiting and headache if it raises the blood-pressure too much. It is contra-indicated in coronary disease, severe vascular disease, hypertension and hyperthyroidism. Applied as spray to the nose, it can cause a secondary congestion when the decongestant effects have passed off.

6 · Anti-hypertensives

Anti-hypertensives are drugs used to reduce the blood-pressure in cases of essential hypertension. Some drugs (such as clonidine hydrochloride, methyldopa) reduce the activity of the sympathetic system, but how they act is not definitely known. Others (such as guanethidine sulphate, bethanidine sulphate, debrisoquine sulphate) are thought to act by interfering with the liberation of nor-adrenaline at sympathetic nerve-endings on blood-vessels. Two or more anti-hypertensives are sometimes given at the same time in order to produce maximum effect with small, non-toxic doses.

Diuretics are used to supplement the actions of anti-hypertensives. They act by increasing the excretion of sodium, the retention of which keeps the blood pressure high, and some cause a fall in blood pressure by dilating peripheral blood-vessels. Oedema need not be present. Tranquillisers may also be given as they can cause a slight fall in blood pressure by relieving the patient's anxiety.

Regular blood pressure readings should be kept while a patient is having treatment with anti-hypertensives.

Clonidine Hydrochloride

Proprietary names. Catapres, Dixarit.

Dose. 50 mcg three times a day, increasing by 50 mcg until control is achieved.

Actions and uses. It is an anti-hypertensive drug, often used in combination with a diuretic. Sudden stopping of treatment is avoided as it can produce a rapid rise of BP.

Small doses are used to prevent and treat migraine.

Toxic and side effects. Sleepiness, dryness of the mouth, constipation and a temporary retention of sodium can occur. Sudden withdrawal can cause a rise in B.P., insomnia, headache, flushing, sweating and fear.

Labetalol

Proprietary name. Trandate.

Dose. 300–2 400 mg per day, usually divided into 3 doses.
1–2 mg per kilo body weight by intravenous injection.

Actions and uses. It is an anti-hypertensive used in mild and severe hypertension. Given intravenously it produces an immediate fall of BP.

Toxic and side effects. Postural hypotension (fall of BP causing fainting when patient stands up).

Indapamide

Proprietary name. Natrilix.

Dose. 2.5 mg once daily.

Actions and uses. This is a diuretic which in the above dose lowers BP without causing diuresis.

Toxic and side effects. No serious ones known.

Methyldopa

Proprietary name. Aldomet.

Dose. 250 mg twice a day for 2 days; increased every
2 days by 250–500 mg up to a total of 2 000 mg daily.
In emergencies 250–500 mg can be given intravenously.

Actions and uses. It is a powerful anti-hypertensive, which
interferes with the production of nor-adrenaline. As
with other drugs with anti-hypertensive effects, the
dose is increased until the blood-pressure is reduced
to a satisfactory level or toxic signs indicate that the
dose should be reduced and another drug tried.

Toxic and side effects. Some symptoms of postural hypotension (lowering of blood pressure when the patient
stands up) may occur – such as dizziness and light
headedness. Rashes can occur, especially in people with
a history of skin diseases. Nasal congestion, dryness of
the mouth, and gastrointestinal disturbances are slight
side effects which are troublesome but not dangerous.
Drowsiness, listlessness and fluid retention can occur.
More serious side effects are jaundice, parkinsonism,
and depression. The drug is not recommended during
pregnancy for fear it might damage the fetus. It is
contra-indicated in acute hepatitis and acute cirrhosis
of the liver, and should not be used if the patient has
a history of liver disease. The drug may cause the
urine to go dark on standing, but this is not a sign of
poisoning.

Guanethidine Sulphate

Proprietary name. Ismelin.

Dose. 10 mg daily for one week; then increased by 10 mg every 5–7 days, according to the patient's response, up to 100 mg daily in divided doses.

Actions and uses. It is an anti-hypertensive which interferes with the liberation of nor-adrenaline from sympathetic nerve-endings. It is given in increasing doses until the blood-pressure is reduced to a satisfactory level. The patient can develop a tolerance to the drug.

Toxic and side effects. Diarrhoea may be troublesome. A postural hypotension can occur. The drug is contra-indicated in phaeochromocytoma, in which condition it can cause a rise in blood-pressure.

Bethanidine Sulphate

Proprietary name. Esbatal.

Dose. 10 mg three times a day, increasing to 200 mg in divided doses.

Actions and uses. It is an anti-hypertensive drug, which acts by interfering with the liberation of nor-adrenaline. It acts rapidly, producing effects within a few hours and is quickly excreted. A thiazide diuretic and potassium supplements are given at the same time if necessary. Tolerance can develop, higher doses then being necessary.

Toxic and side effects. Diarrhoea can occur. Patients become highly sensitive to adrenaline, amphetamine and similar drugs. It is given cautiously to patients with serious kidney disease, cerebral or coronary atherosclerosis, or a history of mental illness.

Debrisoquine Sulphate

Proprietary name. Declinax.

Dose. Initial dose 20–40 mg, increasing to 30–80 mg.

Actions and uses. It is an anti-hypertensive drug with actions similar to guanethidine and bethanidine.

Toxic and side effects. Giddiness or syncope on standing is due to hypotension and is relieved by reducing the dose. Diarrhoea, malaise, a dry mouth and nasal congestion can occur.

Hydrallazine Hydrochloride

Proprietary name. Apresoline.

Dose. 50–200 mg daily by mouth in divided doses; or 20–40 mg by intravenous drip.

Actions and uses. It is an anti-hypertensive. How it acts is not known. It is particularly used in the treatment of high blood-pressure during pregnancy. As the incidence of side effects is fairly high with large doses, it is usually given in smaller doses in combination with another anti-hypertensive drug.

Toxic and side effects. Nausea, vomiting, tachycardia, flushing, sweating, tingling of fingers and toes, headache, tremor, dizziness, nasal congestion, and redness of the conjunctiva may occur, but they may disappear if treatment is continued. Indications for stopping treatment are swollen joints and a condition resembling lupus erythematosus.

Pempidine Tartrate

Proprietary name. Tenormal.

Dose. 10 mg daily in divided doses, increasing up to 80 mg daily.

Actions and uses. Pempidine is an anti-hypertensive which acts by blocking nerve-impulses in the sympathetic and para-sympathetic ganglia and allowing the peripheral vessels to dilate, so causing the blood-pressure to fall. As it is rapidly excreted it has to be taken six-hourly.

Toxic and side effects. Dryness of the mouth, constipation and blurring of vision can occur; they disappear if the drug is stopped or the dose reduced. It is contra-indicated in shock, severe haemorrhage, renal failure, myocardial ischaemia, cerebral ischaemia, and pyloric stenosis.

Pentolinium Tartrate

Dose. 1 mg injected subcutaneously, increasing gradually until effective.

Actions and uses. It is an anti-hypertensive which acts by preventing the liberation of adrenaline and nor-adrenaline. It is particularly useful in the treatment of hypertensive encephalopathy.

Toxic and side effects. Similar to those of pempidine. The contra-indications are the same.

Mecamylamine Hydrochloride

Proprietary name. Inversine.

Dose. 5 mg daily in divided doses, gradually increasing to a maximum of 60 mg daily.

Actions and uses. It is an anti-hypertensive which acts like pempidine. It has a sustained action and need only be taken twice a day.

Toxic and side effects. Similar to those of pempidine. The contra-indications are the same.

Trimetaphan Camphor-Sulphonate

Proprietary name. Arfonad.

Dose. Given intravenously according to requirements of patients.

Actions and uses. It is an anti-hypertensive drug given by slow intravenous injection when controlled hypotension is required during a surgical operation. It is usually given in solutions of 1 mg per ml. Doses of up to 1 g in 2 hours may have to be given.

Prazosin Hydrochloride

Proprietary name. Hypovase.

Dose. 0.5–20 mg daily, with food, beginning with low dose.

Actions and uses. By reducing the peripheral resistance set up by the arterioles it produces a fall in blood pressure without increasing the heart-rate or cardiac output. It is used for patients with all degrees of renal and essential hypertension.

Toxic and side effects. Dizziness, drowsiness, headache, palpitations, a dry mouth and a rash can occur. Severe postural hypotension does not occur.

Mefruside

Proprietary name. Baycaron.

Dose. For hypertension: initial dose: 25–50 mg daily.
Maintenance dose: 25 mg daily or on alternate days.
For oedema: initial dose: 25–50 mg daily, increasing if necessary to 100 mg daily.
Maintenance: 25 mg daily or on alternate days.

Actions and uses. It is an anti-hypertensive and diuretic, best taken as a single morning dose with a little fluid. Potassium supplements are not usually needed.

Toxic and side effects. It can cause dyspepsia and nausea. It is contra-indicated in hepatic disease and when the blood potassium is low. At present it should not be given during the first 3 months of pregnancy.

Metroprolol Tartrate

Proprietary name. Lopresor.

Dose. For hypertension: 100 mg twice daily, increasing if necessary to 200 mg twice daily.
For angina pectoris: 50–100 mg 2–3 times daily.

Actions and uses. It is used as an anti-hypertensive drug, often in combination with a diuretic, and to improve exercise tolerance and prevent anginal attacks in patients with angina pectoris.

Toxic and side effects. It can cause gastrointestinal upsets and disturbances of sleep, effects which are usually temporary or relieved by a reduction of dose. It is contra-indicated in patients with atrio-ventricular block, digitalis-refractory heart failure, and very slow pulse.
If the patient is to have a general anaesthetic, the anaesthetist should be told the patient is taking the drug.

Diazoxide

Proprietary name. Eudemine.

Dose. 150–300 mg intravenously.

Actions and uses. It dilates arteries and causes a fall of BP within a few minutes. It is difficult to control its effect.

Toxic and side effects. No serious ones known.

Sodium Nitroprusside

Proprietary name. Nipride.

Dose. 0.5–1.5 μg per kilo per minute, administered by constant-infusion pump or micro-drip regulator, the rate being adjusted according to the response.

Actions and uses. It dilates arteries and veins and causes a fall of BP in 1–2 minutes. The infusion bottle should be covered with foil to prevent deterioration by exposure to light.

Toxic and side effects. It is contra-indicated for patients with liver disease.

7 · Peripheral Vaso-dilators

Peripheral vaso-dilators are drugs used to dilate peripheral blood-vessels (i.e. those other than the coronary arteries) by reducing muscular spasm in the arterioles. They may do this by preventing nerve-impulses from passing across synapses in the sympathetic nerve ganglia, by antagonizing the action of nor-adrenaline, or by direct action on muscle. They are used mainly in the treatment of Raynaud's disease, but they can be used in an attempt to open up other vascular channels when a main artery is blocked by arteriosclerosis or a clot.

Tolazoline Hydrochloride

Proprietary name. Priscol.

Dose. 25–75 mg by mouth; or 10–20 mg by intramuscular or intravenous injection.

Actions and uses. It causes dilation of peripheral arterioles and capillaries. It is used in the treatment of vascular diseases to reduce spasm in peripheral blood-vessels.

Toxic and side effects. It can produce nausea, vomiting and diarrhoea. It can produce postural hypotension (the blood-pressure falling sharply when the patient stands up) and the patient should lie down for some time after taking it. It is contra-indicated in coronary artery blocking or other severe disease of the heart, and in patients with peptic ulcer.

Phenoxybenzamine Hydrochloride

Proprietary name. Dibenyline.

Dose. 20–60 mg daily in divided doses.

Actions and uses. It is a vaso-dilator which acts by antagonizing the actions of nor-adrenaline and so causing peripheral vaso-dilatation. It is prolonged in its effects.

Toxic and side effects. It has to be used with care when the patient has had a sympathectomy or is a heart-patient and liable to faint.

Cyclandelate

Proprietary name. Cyclospasmol.

Dose. 200–400 mg four times a day.
    Maintenance dose: 400 mg daily.

Actions and uses. It relaxes the smooth muscle of arterioles and so dilates peripheral, coronary and cerebral vessels. It is used in the treatment of peripheral vascular disturbances occurring in athero-sclerosis, diabetes, thrombo-angiitis obliterans (Buerger's disease), Raynaud's disease, night-cramps and similar conditions, cerebral vascular disorders and coronary insufficiency. Treatment over several weeks may be necessary before improvement is noticed.

Toxic and side effects. Side effects are mild. With high doses, some slight flushing, tachycardia, feelings of weakness, nausea and gastrointestinal disturbance may occur and are relieved by a reduction in dose. It is contra-indicated for patients who have had an acute cerebrovascular accident.

8 · Drug Acting on the Respiratory System

Drugs are used to aid expectoration, to relieve spasm in the bronchial muscles, and to relieve cough. Expectorants are drugs supposed to aid removal of secretion from the bronchial glands, but it is doubtful whether they are more effective than a drink of hot water. Drugs that relieve spasm in the bronchial muscle are of particular value in the treatment of asthma. They are commonly given by inhalation.

Ammonium Chloride

Dose. 300 mg–2 g.

Actions and uses. It irritates the gastric mucous membrane. It is said to act as an expectorant, but it is doubtful whether it has any effect. The same drug (in doses of 3–6 g daily in divided doses) is given before the administration of mersalyl injections.

Toxic and side effects. In large doses it produces nausea and vomiting by irritating the gastric mucous membrane.

Ipecacuanha

Other name. Ipecac.

Dose. Liquid extract: 0.025–0.1 ml.
     Tincture: 0.25–1 ml.
     Prepared ipecacuanha: 25–125 mg.

Actions and uses. It is the dried root of a plant of South and Central America. It irritates mucous membranes and is used as an expectorant. It is prepared as a powder, a liquid extract or a tincture, and is a common ingredient of cough mixtures and tablets.

Toxic and side effects. In large doses it produces nausea, vomiting and diarrhoea. As an emetic, 5–20 ml of the tincture can be used.

Potassium Iodide

Dose. 250–500 mg as an expectorant.

Actions and uses. It stimulates secretion from the mucous glands of the bronchi and is therefore used as an expectorant. It is administered (in doses of 25–50 mg) for 10–14 days before operations on the thyroid gland in order to reduce the blood-flow to the gland.

Toxic and side effects. Large or concentrated doses can produce nausea and vomiting by irritating the mucous membrane of the stomach. Some patients become depressed and develop headache, nasal catarrh or skin rashes.

Codeine Phosphate

Dose. 10–60 mg.

Actions and uses. It is a morphine derivative and a mild analgesic. It neither diminishes bronchial secretion nor depresses very much the respiratory centre in the brain; and it is used, usually in a linctus, to relieve a painful or irritating cough. It can be given in a tablet. It may be used in other conditions for its pain-relieving and sleep-producing actions.

Toxic and side effects. Nausea, vomiting and constipation are uncommon.

Methadone Hydrochloride

Other name. Amidone hydrochloride.

Proprietary name. Physeptone.

Dose. 5–10 mg by mouth or subcutaneous injection.

Actions and uses. It depresses the respiratory centre and is used to relieve cough. It has pain-relieving effects similar to those of morphine.

Toxic and side effects. It can produce nausea, vomiting, faintness and dizziness. As it depresses respiration, it must be used cautiously in respiratory diseases, especially in children. Tolerance and addiction can develop, and it should be given only for short periods.

Pholcodine

Proprietary names. Folcovin, Phocil.

Dose. 5–15 mg.

Actions and uses. It is a morphine derivative used to relieve cough. It is usually prescribed in a linctus, and in proprietary preparations it is frequently combined with other anti-tussives.

Toxic and side effects. It has effects similar to those of morphine, but it does not depress the respiratory centre so much. It is said not to cause constipation. Addiction to it is rare.

Belladonna

Dose. 30–200 mg of prepared belladonna herb.

Actions and uses. It is prepared from the leaves of the belladonna plant (deadly nightshade). It reduces spasm in involuntary muscle, reduces secretion from salivary, bronchial and other glands, and increases the rate of the heart. It is used to reduce bronchial spasm in asthma and whooping cough, to relieve renal and biliary colic, and to relieve intestinal colic. Tincture of belladonna is used in the treatment of bed-wetting because of its action in relieving muscular tension of the bladder-wall; it is given in doses of 0.5 ml nightly increased very gradually until either results are achieved or signs of belladonna poisoning develop.

Toxic and side effects. Signs of over-dosage are: widely dilated pupils, dry skin, mouth and throat, thirst, rapid pulse, a raised temperature, and excitement.

Atropine Sulphate

Other name. Atropine sulfate.

Dose. 0.25–2.0 mg by mouth or by subcutaneous or intramuscular injection.

Actions and uses. Atropine reduces spasm in plain muscle, reduces secretion from salivary, bronchial and other glands, increases the heart-rate, dilates the pupils, paralyses the muscles of accommodation of the eye, and raises intra-ocular pressure. It is used before anaesthetics in order to keep the mouth and bronchial passages dry; to relieve renal and biliary colic; and in the treatment of post-encephalitic parkinsonism. Like belladonna, it is used in the treatment of bed-wetting.

Atropine methonitrate (Eumydrin) is used to relieve the spasm of congenital pyloric stenosis in doses of 0.2–0.6 mg half an hour before feeds.

Toxic and side effects. Similar to those of belladonna.

Sodium Cromoglycate

Actions and uses. It inhibits allergic reactions in the respiratory tract. It is used in the treatment of patients with 'extrinsic' asthma, i.e. those with a history of asthma since childhood, a family history of asthma, seasonal asthma or one known to be provoked by a specific allergen, or with a positive skin test. It is especially useful in the prevention of exercise-provoked asthma. Used regularly during the pollen season, it prevents the eye and nose symptoms of hayfever. In some patients it may prevent adverse reactions to some foods. It is available in several forms:

(a) Intal: a powder in a single-dose cartilage (Spincap) administered through a Spinhaler. Dose: 4 cartilages daily for children and adults; increased up to 8 cartilages daily if necessary.

(b) Intal Compound: combined with isoprenaline sulphate; as Intal.

(c) Lomusol: a solution in a special pack, for the prevention of allergic rhinitis. Dose: 1 squeeze to each nostril 6 times daily for children and adults.

(d) Intal Nebuliser Solution: a solution for those who cannot inhale the powdered forms.

(e) Nalcrom: a powder for the treatment of food allergy and of chronic inflammatory bowel disease (ulcerative colitis, proctitis, proctocolitis) in association with other drugs. Dose: 2 capsules 4 times daily before meals; children 1 capsule 4 times daily.

The manufacturer's instructions should be carefully followed. See also p. 192 and p. 196.

Toxic and side effects. Some irritation of nose and throat can occur. There are no contra-indications.

Salbutamol

Proprietary name. Ventolin.

Dose. Inhalant: 1–2 doses 4-hourly.
   By mouth: 2–4 mg 3 times daily.

Actions and uses. It relieves bronchospasm in asthma, chronic bronchitis and emphysema. It is used as an inhalant in acute bronchospasm.

   In the treatment of status asthmaticus and severe bronchospasm in asthma and bronchitis it can be given subcutaneously or intramuscularly in doses of 500 mcg repeated 4-hourly if required or intravenously in a dose of 250 mcg injected slowly and repeated if necessary.

Toxic and side effects. A fine tremor of the hands has been reported. Peripheral vasodilatation and a slight increase in heart rate can occur with over-doses. Over-dosage is treated cautiously with a beta-blocker drug such as propanolol.

Terbutaline Sulphate

Proprietary name. Bricanyl.

Dose. 5 mg 3 times daily.

Actions and uses. It is a bronchodilator used to reduce bronchospasm in asthma, chronic bronchitis and emphysema.

Toxic and side effects. No serious side effects are known, but it is advised that it should be used cautiously for patients who have myocardial insufficiency, hypertension and hyperthyroidism.

9 · Analgesics

Analgesics are drugs used to relieve pain. They fall mainly into three groups: (1) aspirin (acetylsalicylic acid) and similar drugs, which are used to relieve mild or short-lasting pains and do not produce problems of addiction; (2) opium and its derivatives (especially morphine) and similar synthetic preparations; they are powerful relievers of pain and produce sedation and sleep; they are habit forming and can produce serious addiction; and (3) drugs which relieve pains of certain conditions only, e.g. migraine, trigeminal neuralgia.

Acetylsalicylic Acid

Other name. Aspirin.

Proprietary names. Aspro, Genasprin.

Dose. 300 mg–1 g.

Actions and uses. Aspirin is an analgesic (pain-relieving) and anti-pyretic (fever-reducing) drug. It acts within a few minutes. It relieves headache, toothache, migraine, neuralgic pains, and rheumatic pains. As an anti-pyretic it is used to treat the common cold, influenza, and other mild infections. In larger doses (4–8 g daily in divided doses) it is used to treat rheumatic fever.

Large doses taken regularly may prevent strokes and coronary thromboses.

Toxic and side effects. It can cause gastric irritation and bleeding from the mucous membrane of the stomach. It is contra-indicated for patients with peptic ulcer. Calcium salts of it are less irritating. Some people are very sensitive to aspirin, developing asthma-like attacks, swelling of the mucous membrane of the nose, and rashes. Large doses (which may be taken with suicidal intent) can produce headache, nausea, giddiness, collapse and death. It causes more accidental deaths in young children than any other drug; hyperventilation is a risk in children and adults. As it is suspected of causing damage to the kidneys, it should not be given to patients with acute renal disease or severe impairment of renal function. Taken in pregnancy, it may damage a baby's lung, possibly being a cause of some 'blue babies'.

Sodium Salicylate

Dose. 500 mg–2 g.

Actions and uses. It is an analgesic and anti-pyretic drug.
It reduces body temperature by dilating the blood-
vessels in the skin and causing sweating. It is chiefly
used (in doses of 5–10 g daily) in the treatment of
acute rheumatic fever. The drug has to be taken every
2 to 3 hours, for it is rapidly absorbed and excreted.

Toxic and side effects. Gastric irritation can be produced
to avoid which sodium bicarbonate may be given with
it. Headache, giddiness, impaired vision, delirium and
shortness of breath can be produced, in some people
much more easily than in others. Salicylates do not
have a depressant action on the heart. Given in pregnancy, it can be a cause of neonatal bleeding.

Paracetamol

Other name. Acetaminophen.

Proprietary names. Calpol, Eneril, Panadol, Panok, PCM,
Tabalgin.

Dose. 500 mg–1 g.

Actions and uses. It is an analgesic and anti-pyretic drug.
It is frequently prescribed in compounds with aspirin
and other analgesics.

   Distalgesic is paracetamol combined with dextropro-
poxyphene; it has few advantages over paracetamol
alone.

Toxic and side effects. It does not cause gastric irritation
and haemorrhage.

Mefenamic Acid

Proprietary name. Ponstan.

Dose. 250–500 mg.

Actions and uses. It is an analgesic with anti-inflammatory properties. It is used to relieve headache, toothache and other pains of mild to moderate severity. It does not affect the acidity of the stomach contents. Tolerance and addiction do not develop.

Toxic and side effects. In the recommended doses side effects are slight. A rash can occur. Constipation and abdominal pain have been reported. Prolonged administration of high doses has produced diarrhoea, and if this occurs or the white cell count falls the drug should be stopped. It is used cautiously for patients with renal disease or peptic ulcer; it should not be given to children under 14 years as the dose for children has not been established.

Diflunisal

Proprietary name. Dolobid.

Dose. 250 mg once or twice daily.

Actions and uses. It is a non-steroid, anti-inflammatory drug related to aspirin. It is used for the relief of pain and headache.

Toxic and side effects. Nausea and epigastric pain can occur. It is contra-indicated for a patient with a peptic ulcer as it might produce perforation.

Nefopam

Proprietary name. Acupan.

Dose. 30–60 mg by mouth.
    15–30 mg by intramuscular injection.

Actions and uses. It is an analgesic used for the relief of musculo-skeletal and other pain. It is effective for 4–6 hours.

Toxic and side effects. Insomnia, dryness of mouth, nausea, lightheadedness, nervousness. It should not be used for myocardial infarction and is given cautiously to patients with urinary retention or glaucoma.

Opium

Dose. Powdered opium: 25–200 mg.
    Tincture of opium (laudanum): 0.25–2 ml.
    Camphorated tincture of opium (paregoric): 2–10 ml.

Actions and uses. Opium is a substance obtained from the capsules of a certain species of poppy. It contains a number of alkaloids, including morphine, codeine and papaverine. Powdered opium contains 10 per cent of morphine. The effects of opium in relieving pain and checking diarrhoea are largely due to the actions of morphine. Tincture of opium may be given to relieve pain of an inoperable cancer or other incurable condition. Camphorated tincture of opium may be given to relieve cough. *Dover's powder* (dose: 300–600 mg) contains opium powder and ipecacuanha and is given to relieve febrile conditions.

Toxic and side effects. Opium and its alkaloids are drugs of addiction, and their dispensing and administration have to be rigidly controlled.

Morphine

Other names. Morphine sulphate, morphine hydrochloride, morphia.

Dose. 10–20 mg.

Actions and uses. Morphine sulphate and morphine hydrochloride are the two common salts of morphine. Morphine hydrochloride is usually given in the tincture of chloroform and morphine (Chlorodyne). Morphine sulphate is usually given by injection; it may be combined with hyoscine.

Morphine depresses various functions of the central nervous system. It is a powerful analgesic, induces sleep, and depresses the respiratory and cough centres in the medulla oblongata. It is used to relieve severe pain (especially in incurable conditions), to relieve an irritable cough, and as a pre-operative sedative. In combination with hyoscine it may be given to control severe psychotic excitement.

Toxic and side effects. It can produce nausea and vomiting in some patients. It produces constipation. It is a drug of addiction. The addict becomes tolerant to the drug, requiring more and more of it to produce an effect; he becomes dependent on it; and he develops withdrawal symptoms if he is not given it or cannot get it. He develops severe mental and physical deterioration.

to continue

Diamorphine Hydrochloride

Other name. Heroin.

Dose. 5–10 mg, usually by subcutaneous injection.

Actions and uses. It is a powerful analgesic with effects similar to those of morphine. As it can produce a severe addiction, its use is restricted to the relief of pain and anxiety in inoperable cancers, especially of the lung, and other painful fatal diseases.

Toxic and side effects. It is less liable than morphine to produce vomiting and constipation, but it can produce respiratory depression. The addiction it can produce is worse than that of morphine.

Papaveretum

Proprietary names. Omnopon, Opoidine.

Dose. 10–20 mg by mouth or subcutaneous injection.

Actions and uses. It contains alkaloids of opium, 50 per cent of it being morphine. Its actions and uses are similar to those of morphine.

Toxic and side effects. Similar to those of morphine.

Buprenorphine

Proprietary name. Temgesic.

Dose. 300–600 mcg by injection.

Actions and uses. This is an analgesic related to morphine. It starts to relieve pain in 30–60 minutes and is effective for 6–7 hours. It is used to relieve post-operative pain and pain in terminal illness. It is said to be less constipating than morphine and with less risk of physical dependence.

Toxic and side effects. Nausea, vomiting, drowsiness, sweating, dry mouth, dizziness, respiratory depression.

Pethidine Hydrochloride

Other name. Dolantin.

Dose. 25–100 mg by subcutaneous or intramuscular injection; or 25–50 mg by slow intravenous infusion.

Actions and uses. Its actions are similar to those of morphine, but it is not as effective nor as long-acting as morphine in relieving pain. It may be used pre- and post-operatively and to relieve pain during child-birth.

Toxic and side effects. It can produce nausea, vomiting and dizziness in doses normally used. Intravenous injection may produce a fall in blood pressure. A severe addiction can be produced.

Levorphanol Tartrate

Other name. Levorphan.

Proprietary name. Dromoran.

Dose. 1.5–4.5 mg by mouth; 2–4 mg by subcutaneous or intramuscular injection; or 1–1.5 mg by slow intravenous infusion.

Actions and uses. Similar to those of morphine. It is effective when given by mouth.

Toxic and side effects. Similar to those of morphine. It is a drug of addiction.

Methadone Hydrochloride

Other name. Amidone hydrochloride.

Proprietary name. Physeptone.

Dose. 5–10 mg by mouth or subcutaneous injection.

Actions and uses. Its actions and uses are similar to those of morphine, but being less effective in producing sedation it is not used pre-operatively. It is effective when given by mouth. It can be used in the treatment of morphine addiction as any addiction it may produce is less severe than that produced by morphine.

Toxic and side effects. Similar to those of morphine. Acute toxic effects are likely to occur less severely if the patient is lying down when the drug is given. Addiction can occur.

Codeine Phosphate

Dose. 10–60 mg.

Actions and uses. It is a derivative of morphine and
produces only mild sedative and analgesic effects. It is
used in compounds with aspirin in the treatment of
mild infections, being effective in relieving an irritating
cough or slight pains.

    Dihydrocodeine (Proprietary name: D.F. 118) is a
similar drug with similar effects. (Dose: 10–30 mg.)

Toxic and side effects. Toxic and side effects are slight. It
can produce constipation. It does not depress the
respiratory centre or the brain. It does not produce
addiction.

Dipapanone

Proprietary name. Diconal.

Dose. 10–30 mg.

Actions and uses. It is an analgesic with effects similar to
those of morphine. It is given by injection to relieve
severe pain.

Toxic and side effects. Similar to those of morphine. It is
a drug of addiction.

Ergotamine Tartrate

Proprietary name. Femergin.

Dose. 1–2 mg by mouth; or 250–500 mcg by subcutaneous or intramuscular injection.

Actions and uses. It produces constriction of peripheral arterioles. It is used in the treatment of migraine. It is most effective when given by injection at the onset of an attack. Given by mouth it acts slowly and less effectively. It can be given as an inhalant, when it acts quickly, or by suppository to patients who vomit during an attack.

Toxic and side effects. Nausea and vomiting can occur. Prolonged use of high doses can cause the signs and symptoms of ergot poisoning, such as spasm of peripheral vessels, gangrene, and psychosis. It is contraindicated in cardiovascular disease and pregnancy. Care should be taken that young children do not take it accidentally for poisoning in them can be fatal.

Methysergide

Proprietary name. Deseril.

Dose. 4–12 mg daily in divided doses.

Actions and uses. It is sometimes used for the relief of migraine. It does not relieve headaches from other causes.

Toxic and side effects. It can produce nausea, vomiting, diarrhoea, drowsiness, and pain in the legs and groins. It can produce constriction of arteries, and is contraindicated in cardiovascular disease, in pregnancy, and when a patient has oedema.

Pentazocine

Proprietary name. Fortral.

Dose. 30–60 mg by subcutaneous, intramuscular or intravenous injection; up to 180 mg in 24 hours.

Actions and uses. It is a strong analgesic, as powerful as morphine in relieving pain. It produces slight drowsiness. It is said not to produce addiction. It is used to relieve any acute or chronic pain, and in obstetrics to relieve pain in the 1st stage of labour.

Toxic and side effects. Drowsiness, nausea, vomiting can occur; a patient given it should be warned not to drive a car or operate machinery. It can produce respiratory depression. It is contra-indicated in raised intracranial pressure, head-injury, pathological brain conditions, epilepsy, and for patients who are taking a MAOI anti-depressant drug. It is not recommended for children or during pregnancy.

Carbamazepine

Proprietary name. Tegretol.

Dose. 200 mg–1.6 g daily in divided doses.

Actions and uses. It appears to have a specific effect in relieving the pain of trigeminal neuralgia. The dose is gradually increased until pain is relieved. Treatment has to be continued for several months or indefinitely for some patients.

　　The drug is an anti-convulsant and has been used for major and temporal lobe epilepsy.

Toxic and side effects. Side effects are a pink rash, gastro-intestinal upsets, dryness of the mouth, drowsiness, giddiness, and double-vision. If a rash appears, the drug is stopped and not used again. Aplastic anaemia has occurred. As its effects on a fetus are not known, it should not be taken by a woman who might be pregnant. There is no specific antidote for an overdose.

10 · Hypnotics

Hypnotics are drugs used to produce sleep. Members of the barbiturate group (e.g. amylobarbitone sodium, butobarbitone) have commonly been used and are very effective in producing sleep by reducing activity in brain cells at all levels, but they are less used now because they can cause confusion, especially in old people, can become drugs of addiction, can cause death by depressing the respiratory and circulatory centres, and by interfering with liver function can have serious interactions with other drugs. Their withdrawal after prolonged administration can produce restlessness, tremor, confusion and fits. They are being replaced by other drugs (e.g. nitrazepam) which depress the reticular system of the brain without depressing the respiratory and circulatory centres. Other hypnotics are still used, such as chloral hydrate and its derivatives.

Choral Hydrate

Dose. 300 mg–2 g.

Actions and uses. It is a hypnotic, produces sleep within about half an hour and maintains it for about 6 to 8 hours. In therapeutic doses it does not cause cardiac or respiratory depression.

Toxic and side effects. It has a disagreeable taste and may make some patients sick, especially if it is not diluted. After-effects, such as headache and giddiness, occur occasionally. A state resembling alcohol intoxication can be produced. Sudden withdrawal can cause restlessness, tremor, confusion and fits.

Dichloralphenazone

Proprietary name. Welldorm.

Dose. 600 mg–1.8 g.

Actions and uses. It is a combination of chloral hydrate and phenazone, a pain-reliever. This combination enables a small dose of chloral hydrate to be effective in producing sleep when a patient has pain or discomfort.

Glutethimide

Proprietary name. Doriden.

Dose. 250–500 mg.

Actions and uses. It is a hypnotic with moderate effects, producing sleep which lasts for about 6 hours.

Toxic and side effects. Nausea and purpura can occur. Sudden withdrawal can cause restlessness, confusion and tremors.

Paraldehyde

Dose. 2–8 ml by mouth or intramuscular injection.

Actions and uses. It is a strong but safe hypnotic, and can be safely given to people with cardiac disease or other severe physical illness. Its chief disadvantages are its unpleasant taste and smell, which are difficult to mask but are least noticed if given with an equal amount of liquid extract of liquorice. It can be given by intramuscular injection, but it may produce severe pain or an abscess at the site of injection, and care must be taken when injecting it deeply not to inject it into a nerve-trunk. It may be given intramuscularly for delirium tremens, other confusional states, and status epilepticus.

Toxic and side effects. Alcoholics can become addicted to it, taking it as a substitute for alcohol or in addition to alcohol. On long standing it decomposes to acetic acid, an injection of which can be fatal.

Chlormethiazole

Proprietary name. Heminevrin.

Dose. 1–2 g (see below).
Intravenous injection of 0.8 per cent solution.

Actions and uses. It is a sedative, hypnotic and anti-
convulsant. It is used to control senile anxiety, agitation
and confusion, and in the treatment of delirium tremens
(in doses of 1–2 g 2-hourly until effective, in the
withdrawal phase in the treatment of chronic alcoholism
(1–2 g at night), and in the treatment of myoclonic
epilepsy and status epilepticus. It may be combined
with a barbiturate or a tranquillizer.

Toxic and side effects. High doses can cause a fall of
blood-pressure. Patients may complain of tingling in
the nose.

Triclofos

Dose. 1 g at night.

Actions and uses. It is a non-barbiturate sedative and
hypnotic. It is used as a hypnotic for old people and
as a daytime sedative for excitable and disturbed
children.

Toxic and side effects. None known.

Nitrazepam

Proprietary name. Mogadon.

Dose. 5–10 mg in evening (effects may not take place for several hours); 2.5–5 mg for elderly patients.

Actions and uses. It is described as a 'sleep-inducing agent', said to act on the 'emotional centres' of the brain and to separate from emotional stimuli the centres that maintain wakefulness. It is claimed for it that sleep is natural, that the patient can be awakened easily and go to sleep again, and that there is no 'hang-over'. It is used when insomnia is the result of anxiety, stress and depression.

Toxic and side effects. None known. Alcohol should not be taken with it. Its use is not recommended in pregnancy.

Temazepam

Proprietary names. Euhypnos, Normison.

Dose. 10–30 mg at night.

Actions and uses. It is a non-barbiturate hypnotic with a relatively short action. It is unsuitable for depressed patients who wake early.

Toxic and side effects. Drowsiness. Effects of alcohol can be increased. Patient should be warned about driving and operating dangerous machinery the next morning.

Triazolam

Proprietary name. Halcion.

Dose. 0.25 mg.

Actions and uses. It is a non-barbiturate hypnotic with a fairly low incidence of hangover effects.

Toxic and side effects. Drowsiness, dizziness and unsteadiness can occur. A psychotic reaction (severe anxiety, depersonalization, ideas of unreality, delusions, etc.) has occurred in patients treated with high doses for a long time.

Amylobarbitone Sodium

Other name. Soluble amylobarbitone.

Proprietary names. Dorminal, Sodium Amytal.

Dose. 100–200 mg.

Actions and uses. It is a popular and generally safe barbiturate of medium-grade activity. It acts rapidly, produces sleep of 6–8 hours' duration, and has few after-effects. It is used in the treatment of insomnia and as a pre-operative sedative given the night before operation. It does not relieve pain, and when insomnia is due to pain the drug has to be combined with aspirin or another analgesic. It is given intravenously in narco-analysis (psychological analysis in which drugs are used to reduce inhibitions), and in the treatment of convulsions due to drug-intoxication.

Toxic and side effects. The toxic and side effects are those of any barbiturates. Some patients develop excitement before falling asleep. Skin rashes can be produced in some patients. Large doses can produce cardiac and respiratory failure, coma and death. The effects of a barbiturate are increased by alcohol, and the two must never be taken together. Chronic poisoning by repeated doses produces apathy, depression, loss of memory, lack of concentration, and blurring of consciousness.

Butobarbitone

Other name. Butethal.

Proprietary names. Soneryl, Neonal.

Dose. 100–200 mg.

Actions and uses. It is a barbiturate of medium-grade activity. Its actions and uses are similar to those of amylobarbitone.

Toxic and side effects. Similar to those of amylobarbitone.

Cyclobarbitone Calcium

Other name. Cyclobarbital.

Proprietary name. Phanodorm.

Dose. 100–400 mg.

Actions and uses. It is a short-acting and mild hypnotic of the barbiturate group used for mild insomnia.

Toxic and side effects. It is generally safe, but toxic effects similar to those of any barbiturate can be produced in people sensitive to it or when an overdose is taken.

Pentobarbitone Sodium

Other names. Soluble pentobarbitone, pentobarbital sodium.

Proprietary name. Nembutal.

Dose. 100–200 mg.

Actions and uses. It is a hypnotic of the barbiturate group. It acts rapidly and produces deep sleep, but its action is relatively short. It is of special value when the patient's difficulty is in getting off to sleep. It is used intravenously to treat convulsions due to drug poisoning.

Toxic and side effects. Similar to those of amylobarbitone. Liver damage can be produced by prolonged administration.

Quinalbarbitone Sodium

Other names. Secobarbital sodium, sodium secobarbital.

Proprietary name. Seconal Sodium.

Dose. 100–200 mg.

Actions and uses. It is a short-acting hypnotic of the barbiturate group. It is useful for a patient who has difficulty in getting off to sleep.

Toxic and side effects. Similar to those of amylobarbitone.

11 · Anti-convulsants

Anti-convulsants are drugs used to prevent or stop epileptic fits. They fall into two groups: (a) those used to control major fits (grand mal), temporal lobe fits (psycho-motor epilepsy) and jacksonian fits, and (b) those used to control minor fits. Among those in the first group are phenobarbitone, phenytoin sodium, primidone, sulthiame and Nydrane. Among those in the second are ethosuximide, troxidone and paramethadione.

The aim of drug treatment in epilepsy is the achievement of the maximum anti-convulsive effect with the minimum of toxic effects. The correct dose of an anti-convulsant drug for an individual patient is the one that can achieve this for him. Several drugs may have to be tried before an effective one is found. One type of drug alone may not be able to control fits, and it is not unusual for a patient to be taking more than one at a time. Except when acute serious toxic effects are produced, no drug must be stopped abruptly, because of a danger of increasing the number of fits or of precipitating an attack of status epilepticus. Any change must take at least a fortnight, the dose of the old drug being reduced as the dose of the new is increased.

It is not usually necessary for an anti-convulsant drug to be taken more than twice a day. In some patients the epilepsy may be well controlled by a single daily dose. It is generally considered advisable for a patient to have been fit-free for two years before an attempt is made to take him off drugs completely, and even then any attempt at reduction must be made very slowly.

As anti-convulsants can produce a folic acid anaemia, a supplement of folic acid 100 micrograms daily should be taken by mouth.

Phenobarbitone

Other name. Phenobarbital.

Proprietary names. Luminal, Gardenal.

Dose. Adults: 30–120 mg.
    Children up to 1 year: 15–30 mg.
    Children 1–5 years: 30–60 mg.
    Children over 5 years: as for adults.

Actions and uses. It is a depressant of the cerebral cortex and of the reticular formation in the brain-stem.

It is the drug of first choice for major fits (grand mal). It is less effective in the treatment of temporal lobe fits and jacksonian fits.

Toxic and side effects. It is generally a safe drug well tolerated by adults and children. Some lethargy and drowsiness occurring early in treatment may pass off spontaneously. When these symptoms occur late in treatment amphetamine sulphate may be given in doses of 5–20 mg; as well as relieving these symptoms, amphetamine possibly has anti-convulsant properties of its own. The dosage of the drug should be reduced if the patient develops sleepiness, giddiness, blurring of vision or ataxia. The drug should be stopped if the patient develops an allergic rash or megaloblastic anaemia.

Phenytoin Sodium

Other name. Soluble phenytoin.

Proprietary names. Epanutin, Dilantin.

Dose. 50–200 mg daily in divided doses.
100–300 mg intravenously for status epilepticus.

Actions and uses. It reduces EEG abnormalities and is believed to stop the spread of abnormal electrical discharges in the brain. It is used in the treatment of major fits (grand mal) and of focal attacks starting in the cerebral cortex. It is not used in the treatment of minor fits (petit mal), for it may actually increase the number of them. It can be given intravenously in doses of 100–300 mg in the treatment of status epilepticus; as the drug is excreted rapidly, the injection may have to be repeated.

As it seems to reduce sensory impulses passing along nerves, it has been used in the treatment of trigeminal neuralgia.

Toxic and side effects. Minor toxic effects, for which the drug need not be stopped, are gastric upsets (prevented by taking the drug with meals), nervousness and unsteadiness. Hypertrophy of the gums may occur, the gums growing over the teeth; it is disfiguring but not dangerous; it can be prevented to some extent by good dental hygiene and daily massage of the gums; when it is very severe, gingevectomy (excision of the gums) is performed. Excessive growth of hair can occur on the face.

More serious toxic effects, for which the drug should be stopped, are: (a) allergic reactions such as fever, joint swellings, a measles-like rash, enlarged lymph-nodes, enlarged liver and spleen, and exfoliative dermatitis; (b) a cerebellar syndrome characterized by giddiness, ataxia, nystagmus and difficulty in speaking; and (c) a myasthenia gravis-like syndrome. Given in pregnancy it can cause fetal anaemia. It is given cautiously to patients with liver disease.

Primidone

Proprietary name. Mysoline.

Dose. 750–1500 mg daily in divided doses.

Actions and uses. Primidone is chemically related to phenobarbitone and probably acts in the way that drug does by depressing the cerebral cortex and the reticular formation in the brain-stem. It is used for major fits (grand mal), jacksonian fits, and temporal lobe fits (psychomotor epilepsy). It has no effect on minor fits (petit mal). It is probably less effective than phenobarbitone.

Toxic and side effects. Toxic effects are liable to develop before full control is reached. The drug should be reduced in dosage or stopped altogether if drowsiness, giddiness, vomiting, ataxia or confusion develop. It should be stopped if the patient develops megaloblastic anaemia.

Sulthiame

Proprietary name. Ospolot.

Dose. 100–600 mg daily in divided doses.

Actions and uses. It is used in the treatment of major fits, temporal lobe (psychomotor) epilepsy and jacksonian fits. Its effects are uncertain: some patients respond well to it while others show little or no improvement. Because of the uncertainty of its effects, it is not usually used as the drug of first choice for any kind of epilepsy, and it is usually given to patients whose epilepsy has proved resistant to other anti-convulsants.

Toxic and side effects. Some tingling of the hands, feet and face may occur. Other mild toxic effects are headache, blurring of vision, breathlessness and nausea. Much more serious side effects (for which the drug is stopped) are ataxia, drowsiness, confusion, psychosis (schizophrenic or depressive), giddiness, difficulty in swallowing, vomiting and renal damage.

Beclamide

Proprietary name. Nydrane.

Dose. Adults: up to 3 g daily in divided doses.
   Children: one-quarter to one-half the adult dose.

Actions and uses. It is used for major fits and temporal lobe fits. It is said to be particularly useful for epileptics with disturbed behaviour or a psychosis.

Toxic and side effects. Rashes can occur.

Sodium Valproate

Proprietary name. Epilim.

Dose. Adults: 400 mg–1.2 g daily in divided doses.
   Children 0–3 years: 20–30 mg per kilo per day.
   Children 3–15 years: from 400 mg daily.

Actions and uses. It differs in chemical composition from other anti-convulsants. It is used in the treatment of major, minor, focal and temporal lobe epilepsy, either alone or in combination with other anti-convulsants.

Toxic and side effects. Gastric upsets can occur at the start of treatment. Drowsiness, nausea and vomiting can occur. It can potentiate the action of barbiturates and some tranquillisers. It should not be given to pregnant women.

Ethosuximide

Proprietary names. Zarontin, Emeside.

Dose. Adults and children over 6 years: up to 2 g daily in divided doses.

Children under 6 years: up to 250 mg daily in divided doses.

Actions and uses. It is an anti-convulsant of the succinimide group. Little is known of its actions. It is used in the treatment of minor fits, for which it is the drug of first choice. It has no effect on major fits – or possibly increases their number, and when a patient has major fits as well as minor fits, it is advisable to combine it with phenobarbitone or another anti-convulsant acting on major fits. Withdrawal of the drug after it has succeeded in reducing or abolishing fits may not be followed by an increase in them.

Toxic and side effects. Nausea, gastric upsets, dizziness and headache are minor toxic effects, which disappear with a reduction in the dose. More serious toxic effects – such as liver damage, renal damage and aplasia of the bone-marrow – have been rare; if they occur, the drug should be stopped.

Troxidone

Other name. Trimethadione.

Proprietary name. Tridione.

Dose. Adults: 900 mg–1.8 g daily in divided doses.
Children: 600 mg–1.2 g daily in divided doses.

Actions and uses. How it acts on the nervous system is not
known. The EEG wave abnormality (3 per second spike-
and-wave formation), typical of minor epilepsy, may be
reduced or disappear altogether. It is used in the treatment of minor fits and myoclonic epilepsy. It does not
decrease the number of major fits and may actually
increase them.

Toxic and side effects. It is more toxic than ethosuximide.
Minor toxic effects are drowsiness and gastric disturbances. It is liable to produce a troublesome 'glare'
phenomenon in which illuminated objects glitter like
snow in sunshine and for which the patient may have
to wear dark glasses. Baldness can be produced. More
serious complications are a morbilliform or urticarial
dermatitis, aplastic anaemia, agranulocytosis and renal
damage. Monthly examinations of the blood and urine
should be made. Albuminuria, a fall in neutrophils
below 1 600 per cu. mm, or a sharp fall in the number
of platelets are indications for stopping the drug. A
myasthenia-gravis-like syndrome can develop.

Paramethadione

Proprietary name. Paradione.

Dose. Adults: 900 mg–1.8 g daily in divided doses.
Children: 300–900 mg daily in divided doses.

Actions and uses. It is related chemically to troxidone.
Little is known of its actions on the central nervous
system. It is used in the treatment of minor fits only.
It may be tried when troxidone has proved unsuccessful.
It is not usually as effective as troxidone.

Toxic and side effects. The toxic effects are similar to
those of troxidone. The 'glare' phenomenon is less
marked and the sedative effects more marked.

12 · Anti-depressants

Anti-depressants are drugs said to have a specific action on depression.

Imipramine Hydrochloride

Proprietary name. Tofranil.

Dose. For patients under 60 years of age: 75–150 mg daily in divided doses. For patients over 60 years of age: 20–90 mg daily in divided doses.

Actions and uses. How it acts is not definitely known. It is said to have a direct effect on all depressions – of manic-depressive, involutional and reactive type, and on depression produced by physical illness. It reduces depression, anxiety, irritability and peevishness. It is also used to treat enuresis and uncontrolled rheumatic pain.

Toxic and side effects. The drug is suspected of being capable of producing fetal abnormalities and should not be taken by women who might be pregnant.

Toxic effects include atropine-like reactions – dryness of the mouth, disturbance of accommodation of the eyes, constipation, tachycardia, sweating, tremor, tingling, and slight parkinsonism. Disorder of heart action and heart failure can occur. Confusional states can be produced, especially in the elderly. The patient may develop frequency of micturition or have difficulty in starting micturition. Hypotension has occurred. Allergic reactions of the skin – such as erythema, pruritus and urticuria – sometimes occur. Sudden withdrawal can cause anxiety, nausea, dizziness, headache, vomiting and muscular pain.

Amitriptyline

Proprietary names. Laroxyl, Saroten, Tryptizol.

Dose. For patients under 60 years of age: up to 225 mg daily in divided doses. For patients over 60 years of age: up to 90 mg daily in divided doses.

Actions and uses. See imipramine hydrochloride.

Toxic and side effects. Similar to those of imipramine hydrochloride. Acute overdosage may cause fits, a fall of blood-pressure and coma. Gastric lavage should be performed. There is no known antidote.

Nortriptyline

Proprietary name. Aventyl.

Dose. Adults: 20–100 mg daily in divided doses.
Children: 10–75 mg daily in divided doses.

Actions and uses. It is an anti-depressant and tranquillizer, used to treat depression, disturbed behaviour of children and adults, and psychosomatic disorders.

Toxic and side effects. A dry mouth, dizziness, drowsiness and constipation can be produced. The drug has to be used cautiously in patients with any degree of urinary obstruction or glaucoma. It should not be given at the same time as any drug of the MAOI group, and any drug of that group must have been discontinued for at least 10 days before nortriptyline is given.

Protriptyline Hydrochloride

Proprietary names. Concordin, Triptil, Vivactil Hydrochloride.

Dose. 15–60 mg daily in divided doses.

Actions and uses. It is an anti-depressant, producing effects
in 1–5 days. No special dietary restrictions are necessary
as it is not a MAOI drug. It does not produce drowsiness
and patients can continue their usual activities. A
tranquillizer can be given at the same time to relieve
anxiety.

Toxic and side effects. Side effects include tachycardia,
excitement, insomnia, perspiration, abdominal upsets,
allergic skin reactions, dryness of the mouth, blurred
vision, urinary retention and constipation. It is given
cautiously to patients with heart disease. It should not
be given with a MAOI drug, and at least 10 days
should elapse between taking a patient off a MAOI and
putting him on this drug. Contra-indications: enlarged
prostate gland.

Dothiepin Hydrochloride

Proprietary name. Prothiaden.

Dose. 25–50 mg three times a day.

Actions and uses. It is an anti-depressant used for depression, whether or not associated with anxiety.

Toxic and side effects. As for protriptyline hydrochloride.

Clomipramine Hydrochloride

Proprietary name. Anafranil.

Dose. 10–75 mg daily in divided doses or as a single dose at bedtime.

25 mg by intramuscular injection.

Actions and uses. It is an anti-depressant used for all kinds of depression and for obsessional and phobic states. The dose should not be sharply increased for old patients who take the drug in a single dose at bedtime. It can be given by intramuscular injection to severely depressed, uncooperative patients until they are ready to take it by mouth. For severe obsessional and phobic states the dose may have to be increased to 150 mg daily. The drug has some hypotensive action.

Toxic and side effects. Parkinsonian symptoms can be produced. The drug should not be given to epileptic patients as it can induce fits. It has to be used cautiously for patients with oedema, retention of urine or angina pectoris. It is contra-indicated for patients who have had a MAOI drug within 14 days and for patients with liver damage, heart failure or a recent coronary thrombosis.

Phenelzine

Proprietary name. Nardil.

Dose. 15–45 mg daily in divided doses.

Actions and uses. This is one of the drugs commonly referred to as monoamine oxidase inhibitors (MAOI). Amines are chemical substances derived from amino-acids. Compounds with one amine group in them are called monoamines; relatively large amounts of them are found in parts of the brain, as granules in the neurones. Monoamine oxidase inhibitors are so-called because they stop the action of an enzyme called mono-amine oxidase. When this happens the amines accumu-late, possibly causing excitement and increased activity. This is said to be how these drugs act on depression, but there is no direct evidence of this.

The drug can be used for depressions of any type.

Toxic and side effects. Nausea, vomiting, drowsiness and headache are mild toxic effects. Jaundice can occur.

A more serious effect of this group of drugs is their power to increase the actions of other drugs, such as morphine, pethidine and drugs of the imipramine group. Excitement, hyperthermia, and coma have followed the administration of these drugs to patients taking a MAOI, and a patient taking a MAOI should not be given them. Anti-parkinsonian drugs may also be 'potentiated', and drugs of the two types should not be given to the same patient. Hypertensive crises with severe headache, strokes and death have followed the taking of alcohol, cheese, yoghurt, broad beans, Bovril and Marmite and the administration of amphetamine compounds, adrenaline, nor-adrenaline and ephedrine: none of these should be taken by a patient taking a MAOI. The 'potentiating' effects may persist for several weeks after the patient has stopped taking the anti-depressant. It is advisable that a patient taking a drug of this type should carry a card stating so.

Iproniazid

Proprietary name. Marsilid.

Dose. 50–150 mg daily in divided doses.

Actions and uses. This is a MAOI. Its actions are similar to those of phenelzine. It is used for depressions of any type.

Toxic and side effects. Similar to those of phenelzine.

Isocarboxazid

Proprietary name. Marplan.

Dose. 10–30 mg daily in divided doses.

Actions and uses. This is a MAOI. Its actions are similar to those of phenelzine. It is used for depressions of any type.

Toxic and side effects. Similar to those of phenelzine.

Tranylcypromine

Proprietary name. Parnate.

Dose. 10 mg 2–3 times a day.

Actions and uses. It is a MAOI drug used in the treatment of depression. A response within 3 days of beginning treatment can be expected. *Parstelin* is a preparation of Parnate combined with Stelazine for use when anxiety is a marked feature of a depression.

Toxic and side effects. The usual dietary precautions taken with a MAOI drug have to be observed in order to avoid a hypertensive crisis. Other side effects are headache, drowsiness, dizziness, palpitations and a dry mouth. Another anti-depressant should not be taken within a week of beginning or ending treatment with this drug.

Trimipramine

Proprietary name. Surmontil.

Dose. Initial dose: 75 mg daily in divided doses; increased
daily by 25 mg up to a maximum of 400 mg.
  Maintenance dose: 50–150 mg daily in divided doses.
  By injection: 25–50 mg; increased to a maximum of
200 mg daily in divided doses.

Actions and uses. Trimipramine is similar to imipramine.
It is used in the treatment of all kinds of depression,
especially when they are associated with agitation or
anxiety. Treatment may have to be continued for
several months and should not be terminated abruptly.

Toxic and side effects. Dryness of the mouth, dizziness,
drowsiness, blurred vision, confusion and fits have been
reported. The drug must not be given with a MAOI.
It is contra-indicated in glaucoma and any urinary
obstruction.

Doxepin

Proprietary name. Sinequan.

Dose. 30–300 mg daily in divided doses.

Actions and uses. Similar to those of trimipramine.

Toxic and side effects. Similar to those of trimipramine.
It is less likely to cause cardiac irregularity.

Viloxazine

Proprietary name. Vivalan.

Dose. 150–300 mg daily in divided doses with meals.

Actions and uses. It is an anti-depressant used for all types of depression, especially those with severe anxiety. It has no hypnotic effects, and patients remain alert during the day. It is well tolerated by old people and as it has some anti-convulsant properties it is useful for depressed epileptics.

Toxic and side effects. A temporary gastrointestinal upset can occur. If given to an epileptic patient who is taking phenytoin, the dose of phenytoin may have to be reduced.

Lithium Carbonate

Proprietary names. Camcolit, Priadel (slow release).

Dose. Initial dose 250 mg twice daily, increasing up to 1 500 mg in divided doses.

Actions and uses. It is used to treat affective attacks and acts by displacing sodium which is raised in depression and more so in mania. The blood level is checked after 6 days' treatment. When an appropriate dose is found, it can be continued for years. It is sometimes given for 6-day periods only to avoid cumulation.

Toxic and side effects. Nausea, vomiting, deafness, giddiness, tinnitus, paraesthesiae, tremor and diarrhoea can occur; the drug is stopped and salt and fluid are given. A myasthenia-gravis-like syndrome can be produced.
   Damage to the kidney can occur causing impairment of renal function, frequency, and an increase in amount of urine passed. The drug should not be given unless kidney function can be regularly monitored and serum lithium concentrations measured. The patient should not make any major change in diet without medical advice.

13 · Tranquillizers

The tranquillizers are drugs, of varying composition, for which it is claimed that they improve the patient's behaviour, reduce anxiety, tension, agitation and psychotic symptoms, and make him manageable and accessible to other forms of treatment such as psychotherapy.

Chlorpromazine

Proprietary name. Largactil.

Dose. 15–50 mg daily in divided doses by mouth or injection.

In severe psychoses: up to 1 000 mg daily.

Actions and uses. It is a tranquillizer. It reduces over-activity, restlessness and tension without producing depression or any clouding of consciousness. It increases the effects of barbiturates, and given with them enables small doses of barbiturates to produce full clinical effect. It is used in the treatment of over-activity in schizophrenia, manic-depressive states, paranoid psychoses and senile dementia. It is used in the treatment of acute and chronic alcoholism, and to cover the withdrawal of drugs during the treatment of drug addiction. It is used to treat hiccup, nausea, vomiting, pruritus and hyperpyrexia. It can be given by mouth, by deep intramuscular injection, or by suppository. Once it has become effective, treatment can be continued by smaller maintenance doses.

Toxic and side effects. Toxic and side effects include drowsiness (usually at the beginning of treatment and disappearing with the continuation of the drug); weakness; postural hypotension (when the drug is given by injection); an iron-deficiency anaemia, thrombocytopenia, agranulocytosis; parkinsonism (tremor, rigidity, parkinsonian face); jaundice (due to the obstruction of the small canals in the liver), often preceded by fever; urticarial and erythematous skin rashes; and a discharge of milk from the breasts. An acute intoxication can develop if large doses of the drug are given in rapid succession. Patients who have been having large amounts of the drug for a long time may develop a slate-grey discoloration of the skin and tiny opacities in the lens and cornea of the eye. Nurses handling the drug may develop a sensitivity of the skin to it; they should wear rubber gloves when handling any preparation of it. To avoid sensitization, tablets of the drug should not be crushed.

Contra-indications are liver damage, fever, coma, and when drugs known to produce leucopenia (reduction of white blood cells) or postural hypotension are being administered.

Clobazam

Proprietary name. Frisium.

Dose. 10 mg 3 times a day.

Actions and uses. It is a psychotropic drug used for the treatment of anxiety. Two weeks' treatment is necessary before full effects are achieved.

Toxic and side effects. Drowsiness, sedation, dizziness, unsteadiness.

Trifluoperazine

Proprietary name. Stelazine.

Dose. 15–30 mg daily in divided doses by mouth; 1–3 mg daily by intramuscular injection; or 2–4 mg daily for nausea and vomiting.

Actions and uses. Its actions and uses are similar to those of chlorpromazine. It is used in acute and chronic schizophrenia, in acute mania, in psychoses due to organic brain damage, delirium tremens, and for mentally retarded patients showing disturbed behaviour. It produces a decline in compulsive and aggressive behaviour, the fading of hallucinations, the return of mental insight, and a reawakening of old interests. Small doses are used for the treatment of nausea and vomiting.

Toxic and side effects. Drowsiness, increased salivation and parkinsonism can occur. It is contra-indicated in serious heart disease.

Perphenazine

Proprietary name. Fentazin.

Dose. 8–24 mg daily in divided doses; or 5 mg intramuscularly every 6 hours.
  Before operation: 3.75–5 mg intramuscularly 1 hour before operation.

Actions and uses. It is a tranquillizer used mainly in the treatment of anxiety and tension states. It can also be used as a pre-operative tranquillizer and in the treatment of nausea and vomiting.

Toxic and side effects. Toxic and side effects are similar to those of other phenothiazines. It is contra-indicated in leucopenia, coronary artery disease, and congestive heart failure.

Prochlorperazine

Proprietary names. Stemetil, Compazine.

Dose. 125–250 mg daily in divided doses for psychoses and neuroses.

Actions and uses. Its actions and uses are similar to those of trifluoperazine. It is used in the treatment of acute and chronic schizophrenia, anxiety states, acute and chronic alcoholism, narcotic addictions, and presenile and senile psychoses. Once effects have been produced, they may be maintained by a smaller maintenance dose. It is used in small doses (5–25 mg daily) in the treatment of migraine, Ménière's disease and other disorders of the labyrinth of the ear.

Toxic and side effects. Restlessness, insomnia, dryness of the mouth, stuffy nose, and disturbances of visual accommodation can occur. With large doses parkinsonism can be produced. An excitomotor syndrome occurs rarely; it is characterized by tremors, choreoathetoid movements, torticollis, trismus, sweating, rapid pulse-rate, sensory disturbance and abdominal swelling; it is relieved by a reduction in dose or withdrawal of the drug, and by anti-parkinsonian drugs.

Fluphenazine Hydrochloride

Proprietary name. Moditen.

Dose. Adults: 1–20 mg once daily.
  Children: 250 mcg–1 mg once daily.
  Moditen Enanthate: 12.5–25 mg by intramuscular injection every 10–28 days.

Actions and uses. It is a phenothiazine derivative used in the treatment of anxiety states, schizophrenia, senile agitation, and behaviour problems in children. It is a powerful tranquillizer with strong anti-delusional and anti-hallucinatory actions, does not have a sedative effect, and can be used for ambulant patients.
  Moditen Enanthate is a preparation of the drug given intramuscularly. Given at intervals of 10–28 days, it is useful for patients who cannot be trusted to take oral preparations regularly.

Toxic and side effects. Extra-pyramidal (parkinsonian) reactions can be produced when the dose is high and treatment prolonged; anti-parkinsonian drugs should be given to prevent or relieve them. A fall of blood-pressure occurs rarely.
  Injectable preparations of similar drugs are:
  fluphenazine enanthate (Moditen enanthate)
  fluphenazine decanoate (Modecate)
  flupenthixol decanoate (Depixol)
  cis-clopenthixol decanoate (Cloxipol)

Fluspirilene

Proprietary name. Redeptin.

Dose. Initial dose: 2 mg weekly by intramuscular injection, increasing by 2 mg weekly up to 20 mg.

Maintenance dose: 2–8 mg weekly by intramuscular injection.

Actions and uses. It is a long-acting tranquillizer given by intramuscular injection in the treatment of schizophrenia. Its effects last for a week. Once the optimal dose has been established, the effects remain fairly constant.

Toxic and side effects. Extra-pyramidal symptoms can appear within 6 hours of injection and last for about 48 hours; they are controllable by a reduction in dose or the administration of anti-parkinsonism drugs. Drowsiness, blurred vision, nausea, vomiting, dizziness, headache and sweating can occur, and if they become worse can be stopped by omitting 1 in 4–5 weekly injections. It has to be used cautiously with epileptics as it can precipitate a fit.

Pericyazine

Proprietary names. Neulactil, Neuleptil.

Dose. Mild illnesses: 2.5–5 mg midday; 5–10 mg evening.
Severe illnesses: 5–30 mg midday; 10–60 mg evening.
By intramuscular injection: 10–20 mg.

Actions and uses. It is a tranquillizer with effects similar
to those of chlorpromazine. It is about ten times more
active than chlorpromazine. It is used in acute and
chronic schizophrenia, senile dementia, manic-depressive psychosis, severe anxiety states, and other mental
illnesses.

Toxic and side effects. As it can cause sleepiness, the
dose given by day is usually smaller than that given at
night. The dose is much reduced if the patient is
having any other tranquillizer, sedative or hypnotic.
Children and old people may react acutely and should
not be given intramuscular injections. Other toxic or
side effects are nausea, vomiting, diarrhoea, sweating,
tachycardia, postural hypotension, fainting and parkinsonism (tremor, rigidity, parkinsonian face). Patients
on the drug should be advised not to drive cars or
handle dangerous machinery. It should not be taken
by a woman who might be pregnant.

Thioridazine Hydrochloride

Proprietary name. Melleril.

Dose. 30–600 mg daily in divided doses.

Actions and uses. It is a tranquillizer used in the treatment
of anxiety, tension, agitation, emotional disorders and
aggression.

Toxic and side effects. Drowsiness, dizziness, faintness,
dryness of the mouth and nasal stuffiness can occur
but usually pass off.

Chlordiazepoxide Hydrochloride

Proprietary name. Librium.

Dose. 30–100 mg daily in divided doses.

Actions and uses. It is a tranquillizer used in the treatment of anxiety, tension, agitation, obsessional states, alcoholic withdrawal states and emotional complications of organic disease. It is more useful for mild than for severe symptoms. It is of little value in the treatment of schizophrenia. To prevent ataxia, the first dose for patients over the age of 60 should not be higher than 10 mg. It has been used (in doses of 10–30 mg daily) in the treatment of children with school phobia. It has been used in the treatment of children with allergic conditions such as eczema, allergic rhinitis and asthma, and of children with disturbed behaviour.

Toxic and side effects. Drowsiness and ataxia can occur; when this happens the dose should be reduced. Patients should avoid alcohol and not drive cars.

Methylpentynol

Proprietary name. Isomnol.

Dose. 250 mg–1 g.

Actions and uses. It is a tertiary alcohol used in the treatment of tension and mild anxiety states. It is sometimes given as a hypnotic, but as such it is ineffective.

Toxic and side effects. It can cause ataxia and ptosis. People taking it should be warned not to drive a car.

Haloperidol

Proprietary names. Serenace, Haldol.

Dose. 1–over 200 mg daily.

Actions and uses. It is a tranquillizer used to control schizophrenia, mania and severe agitation. It is given by injection when rapid control of an acute mental illness is required.

Toxic and side effects. A parkinsonian-reaction can be produced by big doses and is avoided by giving an anti-parkinsonian drug at the same time. It increases the soporific effects of depressants of the brain. Intramuscular injection is painful.

Trifluoperidol

Proprietary name. Triperidol.

Dose. Initial dose 500 mcg; increased by 500 mcg at 3–4 days' interval until effective. Maximum dose 8 mg.

Actions and uses. It is a tranquillizer used in the treatment of acute schizophrenia and mania.

Toxic and side effects. Slight parkinsonism can occur. It potentiates the effect of morphine and barbiturates.

Oxazepam

Proprietary name. Serenid-D.

Dose. 45–180 mg daily in divided doses.
   Elderly patients: 30 mg daily in divided doses.

Actions and uses. It is a tranquillizer used in the treatment of anxiety, agitation and tension.

Toxic and side effects. It can cause dizziness, drowsiness and headache. Patients taking it should not take alcohol, drive cars or work dangerous machines.

Lorazepam

Proprietary name. Ativan.

Dose. 1–2.5 mg up to 3 times a day.

Actions and uses. It is a tranquillizer used in the treatment of chronic anxiety.

In doses of 2–4 mg it is used as a premedication and as a post-operative sedative.

Toxic and side effects. It is unsuitable for day-care surgery as it can act for 24 hours and cause amnesia. Patients taking it should not drive a car.

Diazepam

Proprietary name. Valium.

Dose. 6–30 mg daily in divided doses by mouth.

0.2 mg per kilo of body-weight (usually 10–20 mg) intravenously.

Actions and uses. As a tranquillizer it is used for anxiety, agitation and tension. As a muscle-relaxant it is used in the treatment of cerebral palsy and muscle-spasm from other causes. It is given intravenously in the treatment of tetanus, status epilepticus, and for various surgical and diagnostic procedures. It is a useful pre-medication in a dose of 10–20 mg orally or intra-muscularly.

Toxic and side effects. Patients should be warned not to take alcohol or to drive cars or use dangerous machines. Large doses depress respiration and circulation.

Thiothixene

Proprietary name. Navane.

Dose. 10–60 mg daily.

Actions and uses. It is a tranquillizer used in the treatment of acute and chronic schizophrenia. It is given as a tablet which dissolves immediately in the mouth and cannot later be spat out.

Toxic and side effects. It can produce a parkinsonian-like effect, hyperactivity, increased pulse-rate and a fall in blood-pressure. As it might precipitate a fit it is used with caution in epileptics. Contra-indication: any disease of the blood.

14 · Anti-parkinsonism Drugs

Paralysis agitans (Parkinson's disease) is a progressive neurological disease. Its clinical features are thought to be the result of an imbalance between an acetyl-choline secreting system and a dopamine-secreting system in the basal ganglia of the brain, with a reduction in the amount of dopamine below the normal.

Treatment can be by:

a *drugs which reduce the amount of acetyl-choline formed*:
benzhexol hydrochloride
benztropine methane-sulphonate
orphenadrine hydrochloride
procyclidine hydrochloride
biperiden hydrochloride
methixene hydrochloride

b *drugs which promote the secretion of dopamine or of substances with a dopamine-like activity*:
levodopa
amantadine hydrochloride

Benzhexol Hydrochloride

Proprietary names. Artane, Pipanol.

Dose. 2–15 mg daily in divided doses.

Actions and uses. It is used in paralysis agitans and acts mainly by reducing the rigidity.

Toxic and side effects. Dryness of the mouth, urinary retention, drowsiness and (with high doses) confusion can occur.

Benztropine Methane-Sulphonate

Proprietary name. Cogentin.

Dose. 500 mcg–6 mg daily in divided doses.

Actions and uses. It is used in the treatment of paralysis agitans. Its actions are similar to those of benzhexol. The initial dose should be 500 mcg. The dose can be gradually increased until the patient is relieved or toxic signs appear. As the drug is liable to be cumulative, the dose is kept small.

Toxic and side effects. As for benzhexol hydrochloride.

Orphenadrine Hydrochloride

Proprietary name. Disipal.

Dose. 100–300 mg daily in divided doses with meals.

Actions and uses. It is used in the treatment of paralysis agitans, drug-induced parkinsonism, presenile and senile depression. It may slightly relieve the depression often present in paralysis agitans.

Toxic and side effects. As for benzhexol hydrochloride.

Procyclidine Hydrochloride

Proprietary name. Kemadrin.

Dose. 7.5–30 mg daily in divided doses with meals.

Actions and uses. It is used in the treatment of paralysis agitans to relieve rigidity and tremor. The initial dose should not be more than 7.5 mg. This drug is usually well tolerated by elderly patients.

Toxic and side effects. It can produce gastric irritation.

Biperidin Hydrochloride

Proprietary name. Akineton.

Dose. 1 mg twice a day, increasing to 4 mg three times a day.

5 mg intravenously or intramuscularly for an oculo-gyric crisis.

Actions and uses. It is used to treat paralysis agitans and parkinsonism due to drugs. It controls rigidity, checks salivation and relieves tremor.

Toxic and side effects. As for benzhexol hydrochloride.

Methixene Hydrochloride

Proprietary names. Tremonil, Tremaril.

Dose. Initial dose: 2.5 mg three times a day.

Maintenance dose: 15–60 mg daily in divided doses.

Actions and uses. It is used to control tremor in paralysis agitans and senility, and to control the extra-pyramidal side effects of tranquillizers.

Toxic and side effects. It can produce blurring of vision and dryness of the mouth, but these usually pass off as treatment is continued. It is contra-indicated in glaucoma, irregularities of the heart, enlargement of the prostate gland, and urinary retention from any cause.

Levodopa

Dose. 0.25 g twice daily, increased weekly up to a total daily dosage of 2.5–5.0 g daily in divided doses.

Actions and uses. It relieves the rigidity and improves the gait and stability in parkinsonism. Tremor is not usually affected. Improvement may not take place for 2–3 months. Because of the severity of its side-effects, it is used when other drugs have failed.

Sinemet is a combination of levodopa with carbidopa, which conserves levodopa for activity in the brain only.

Toxic and side effects. The following can occur and be severe: nausea, vomiting, postural hypotension, confusional states, hallucinatory states, involuntary movements of the lips, tongue, face and jaw, torticollis, athetoid movements of the limbs.

Amantadine Hydrochloride

Proprietary name. Symmetrel.

Dose. 200–600 mg daily.

Actions and uses. It is used in the treatment of paralysis agitans, being especially useful for early cases, in whom it can produce rapid improvement.

Toxic and side effects. Nervousness, insomnia, dizziness fits, feelings of unreality and hallucinations can occur.

15 · Anti-histamines

Anti-histamines are drugs that block the actions of histamine. Histamine is a chemical substance normally present in the tissues. It can become liberated as the result of allergic reactions, producing asthma, hay fever, allergic rhinitis, angio-neurotic oedema, urticaria, pruritus, and anaphylactic reactions. It produces dilatation of capillaries, increased permeability of capillary walls, and spasm of plain muscles. The anti-histamines relieve these manifestations, with the exception of the muscular spasm, being thus of little value in the relief of asthma. They are usually taken by mouth but in emergencies some of them can be injected.

Some of them are used also for the prevention of travel-sickness, of the nausea and vomiting of pregnancy, of irradiation-sickness and of the treatment of parkinsonism.

Special precautions to be taken with anti-histamines are:

a They should not be taken by anyone who is driving a car or about to do so (because of the drowsiness they produce);

b They should not be taken with alcohol (they increase its effects);

c They should not be combined with barbiturates (they increase their effects);

d They should not be taken by epileptics (they can produce fits in epileptics).

There are many drugs in this group. Many of them are chemically related. Individual patients differ in their response to them, and a patient may have to try several in order to find the one that suits him best. Tolerance develops with use and when this happens another drug is tried.

Diphenhydramine Hydrochloride

Proprietary name. Benadryl.

Dose. 25–75 mg by mouth; or 10–50 mg by intramuscular or intravenous injection.

Actions and uses. It is an anti-histamine of moderate potency used in the treatment of allergic reactions. It can also be used in the treatment of parkinsonism and in the prevention of travel sickness, nausea and vomiting of pregnancy, and irradiation-sickness.

Toxic and side effects. Drowsiness occurs commonly with this and most other anti-histamines. It may be sufficiently pronounced as to prevent the use of the drug by day. Dryness of the mouth, headache, giddiness, tinnitus and gastro-intestinal disturbances can occur.

As with all anti-histamines, the special precautions described above must be taken.

Antazoline Hydrochloride

Dose. 50–100 mg.

Actions and uses. Similar to those of diphenhydramine. It is relatively weak and effective for only 3–4 hours.

Toxic and side effects. Similar to those of diphenhydramine.

Chlorcyclizine Hydrochloride

Dose. 50–200 mg.

Actions and uses. Similar to those of diphenhydramine. It is effective over a longer period.

Toxic and side effects. Similar to those of diphenhydramine.

Chlorpheniramine Maleate

Proprietary name. Piriton.

Dose. Adults: 2–4 mg by mouth; or 5–10 mg by subcutaneous, intramuscular or slow intravenous injection.
Children: 1–2 mg by mouth.

Actions and uses. It is a powerful anti-histamine, which
can be injected when rapid action is required.

Toxic and side effects. Drowsiness and giddiness may occur.

Meclozine Hydrochloride

Dose. 25–50 mg.

Actions and uses. Similar to diphenhydramine.

Toxic and side effects. Similar to diphenhydramine.

Mepyramine Maleate

Proprietary name. Anthisan.

Dose. 50–100 mg; or 25–50 mg by intramuscular or intravenous injection.

Actions and uses. Similar to those of diphenhydramine.

Toxic and side effects. Similar to diphenhydramine.

Phenindamine Tartrate

Proprietary name. Thephorin.

Dose. 25–50 mg.

Actions and uses. It is an anti-histamine, but unlike other
anti-histamines it has a stimulating and not depressive
effect on the brain and does not produce drowsiness.

Toxic and side effects. Similar to diphenhydramine, except
that it does not produce drowsiness.

Promethazine Hydrochloride

Proprietary name. Phenergan.

Dose. Adults: 20–75 mg at night; or 20–25 mg by deep intramuscular injection.
  Children: 10 mg at night.

Actions and uses. It is a strong anti-histamine with a prolonged action.

Toxic and side effects. It is so liable to produce drowsiness that it should be given only at night.

Triprolidine Hydrochloride

Proprietary names. Actidil, Pro-Actidil.

Dose. Adults: 2.5–10 mg.
  Children: 500 mcg–1 mg.

Actions and uses. It is a powerful anti-histamine. It maintains its effects for up to 8 hours. It should preferably be given at night only, especially if a large dose is taken. *Pro-Actidil* is a slow-release tablet active for up to 24 hours.

Toxic and side effects. As for diphenhydramine.

Cyclizine Hydrochloride

Proprietary name. Valoid.

Dose. 25–50 mg by mouth; or 50–100 mg by rectum.

Actions and uses. It is an anti-emetic drug with anti-histamine properties. It is used to prevent or treat sea-sickness, air-sickness, irradiation-sickness, and Ménière's disease. The dose should not be repeated more than twice in 24 hours.

Toxic and side effects. Dry mouth, drowsiness and blurred vision can occur.

Dimenhydrinate

Proprietary names. Dramamine, Gravol.

Dose. 50–100 mg by mouth; or 25–50 mg by intramuscular injection.

Actions and uses. It is an anti-emetic drug with anti-histamine properties. It is used to prevent or treat sea-sickness, air-sickness, radiation-sickness, vomiting of pregnancy, and Ménière's disease.

Toxic and side effects. Drowsiness can occur.

Promethazine Theoclate

Proprietary name. Avomine.

Dose. 25–50 mg daily.

Actions and uses. It is an anti-emetic drug with anti-histamine properties. It is used to prevent and treat sea-sickness, air-sickness, radiation-sickness, vomiting of pregnancy and Ménière's disease. To prevent travel-sickness a dose should be taken the night before travelling.

Toxic and side effects. Drowsiness can occur.

16 · Stimulants of the Nervous System

Some stimulants of the nervous system (e.g. bemegride) are used mainly for their action in stimulating the respiratory and vasomotor centres of the brain in cases of poisoning by barbiturates or other narcotic drugs.

Bemegride

Proprietary name. Megimide.

Dose. 50 mg intravenously; repeated, if necessary, every 10 minutes until 1 g has been given.

Actions and uses. It is a stimulant of the vasomotor and respiratory centres of the brain. It is given intravenously in the treatment of barbiturate poisoning and chloral hydrate poisoning.

Leptazol

Other name. Pentetrazole.

Dose. 50–100 mg by injection.

Actions and uses. It is a stimulant of the vasomotor and respiratory centre of the brain. It can be given by subcutaneous, intramuscular or intravenous injection. It is used in the treatment of barbiturate poisoning or poisoning by other narcotic drugs.

Toxic and side effects. A large dose given intravenously can produce a fit.

Nikethamide

Dose. 2–8 ml by intravenous injection.

Actions and uses. It stimulates the respiratory centre in the medulla oblongata of the brain, and increases both the depth and the rate of respiration. It has been used in the treatment of barbiturate poisoning or poisoning by other narcotic drugs. Its effects are short, and it has largely been replaced by bemegride and leptazol.

Toxic and side effects. Large doses can produce convulsive movements.

Levallorphan

Proprietary name. Lorfan.

Dose. 200 mcg–2 mg by intravenous injection.

Actions and uses. It is a respiratory stimulant and an antidote to morphine. It is used in the treatment of poisoning by morphine, pethidine and similar drugs. It is ineffective in poisoning by other narcotic drugs.

Nalorphine

Dose. 5–10 mg by intravenous injection.

Actions and uses. Similar to levallorphan.

Micoren

Proprietary name. Micoren.

Dose. 400 mg 3–4 times a day.

Actions and uses. It stimulates respiration by acting directly on the respiratory centre in the brain, increasing the depth of respiration and improving gaseous exchanges. It is used in the treatment of chronic bronchitis and other conditions in which there is respiratory insufficiency.

Toxic and side effects. Rashes and gastrointestinal disturbances can occur. It is used with caution in epileptics because it might produce a fit.

17 · Drugs Acting on the Alimentary Tract

The drugs most commonly used in the treatment of diseases of the stomach are those to neutralize acid; this is desirable in the treatment of hyper-chlorhydria (excessive secretion of hydrochloric acid). Several drugs (such as magnesium trisilicate) are now available which will do this effectively and without producing an excessive secretion of acid later. The muscular spasm associated with a peptic ulcer may be relieved by belladonna, by its derivative atropine, or by similar synthetic drugs with anti-spasmodic actions.

A number of drugs are used as *carminatives*, i.e. drugs that cause the patient to belch. Among these are sodium bicarbonate and oil of peppermint. They are little used today. Other drugs are called *bitters*; they are supposed, by their bitterness, to stimulate the flow of gastric juice and increase appetite; their value is doubtful.

Aluminium Hydroxide Gel

Other name. Aluminium hydroxide.

Proprietary names. Alocol, Aludrox.

Dose. 7.5–15 ml.

Actions and uses. It is an antacid used in the treatment of hyper-acidity of the stomach and of peptic ulcer. It is given in milk or water every 2–4 hours, by mouth or by a gastric drip, or in tablets to be chewed. It may be combined with other antacids (e.g. light magnesium carbonate, magnesium trisilicate).

Toxic and side effects. It prevents the absorption of tetracycline antibiotics and should not be used when they are being given. It is constipating.

Magnesium Trisilicate

Dose. 500 mg–2 g.

Actions and uses. It is a slowly acting antacid and adsorbent drug used in the treatment of hyper-acidity of the stomach and peptic ulcer. It may be combined with other antacids (e.g. aluminium hydroxide gel) and anti-spasmodics (e.g. belladonna).

Toxic and side effects. Some purging or diarrhoea may be caused.

Magnesium Hydroxide

Dose. 500 mg–4 g.

Actions and uses. It is frequently prescribed as a magnesium hydroxide mixture (Cream of Magnesia). It has laxative effects.

Toxic and side effects. Overdosage can produce diarrhoea.

Sodium Bicarbonate

Other name. Baking Soda.

Dose. 1–5 g.

Actions and uses. It neutralizes acid in the stomach. It may be given with gentian or other bitters as a supposed aid to appetite.

It may be applied in dilute solution to the skin to relieve itching. A 1 per cent solution may be used to wash out the eye. As it softens wax it may be used in a weak solution to syringe out the ear.

Toxic and side effects. Excessive consumption can produce alkalosis.

Calcium Carbonate

Dose. 1–4 g.

Actions and uses. It is used as an antacid and causes the patient to belch. As it is constipating it may be given in a mixture with magnesium oxide or magnesium carbonate, which are purging.

Toxic and side effects. Taken in excessive quantities it can increase the amount of calcium in the blood.

Carbenoxolone Sodium

Proprietary names. Biogastrone; Duogastrone (for duodenal ulcers).

Dose. 50–100 mg three times a day after meals.

Actions and uses. It is a drug obtained from liquorice. It is anti-inflammatory and is used in the treatment of peptic ulcer, whose healing it promotes, possibly by stimulating the secretion of excessive amounts of mucus. A dose of 50 mg is advisable for patients over 60 years of age or with renal or cardiac disease. If 'heartburn' occurs, the drug should be taken in milk.

Toxic and side effects. 'Heartburn', headache, shortness of breath and lassitude may occur. Retention of sodium and water can cause increase in weight. Caution is exercised if the patient has heart disease for the increase in weight might lead to heart failure. Large doses can produce hypertension.

Polymethylsiloxane

Proprietary name. Asilone.

Dose. 250–500 mg sucked or chewed before meals and at bedtime. Suspension 5–10 ml.

Actions and uses. A protective coat of the drug forms over the mucous membrane of oesophagus and stomach; gas and ingested air are evacuated from the stomach and peristalsis is stimulated. The drug is used to relieve oesophagitis due to hiatus hernia, and to relieve flatulence and gastritis.

Toxic and side effects. Minor bowel disturbances can occur.

Benzylonium Bromide

Dose. 5–30 mg.

Actions and uses. It is an anti-cholinergic drug used in the treatment of peptic ulcer. It reduces the amount and acidity of gastric juice and reduces gastrointestinal movements. 'Slow-release' preparations are particularly useful in reducing peptic-ulcer pain at night. Other methods of treating ulcers (by diet, antacids, sedation, etc.) are continued.

Toxic and side effects. Side effects are usually slight. They include mild blurring of vision, heartburn, dryness of the mouth, constipation and difficulty in micturition.

Cimetidine

Proprietary name. Tagamet.

Dose. 1 g daily (in doses of 200 mg 3 times a day, 400 g at bedtime) for 6 weeks.

Maintenance dose: 400 mg 1–2 times a day.

Actions and uses. It reduces gastric secretion acid and is used in the prevention and treatment of duodenal ulcer and in the treatment of gastric ulcer. It relieves symptoms and promotes healing. Maintenance doses are necessary for 3–6 months. Longer treatment may have to be given to patients who relapse after that and are not fit for surgery.

It is also used in the treatment of gastro-oesophageal reflex, gastrointestinal haemorrhage, Zollinger-Ellison syndrome and malabsorption.

Toxic and side effects. In short term treatment no serious side effects are known. In long term treatment confusion can occur in old people or patients with impaired renal function.

Metoclopramide

Proprietary name. Maxolon.

Dose. 10–20 mg.

Actions and uses. It is an anti-emetic drug. It is not
chemically related to the anti-histamines and the phenothiazines. It acts locally on the stomach and centrally
on the vomiting centre in the brain. It is used to reduce
vomiting in gastrointestinal disorders, malignant
disease, uraemia, congestive heart failure, post-operative
conditions and in deep X-ray and cobalt treatment. It
is used in diagnostic radiology of the stomach when it
is necessary to hasten gastric emptying in gastric stasis,
to reduce spasm in the duodenal cap, or to prevent
nausea or vomiting during barium meal examination.

Toxic and side effects. Some extra-pyramidal symptoms
can appear within 36 hours of starting treatment:
spasm of the facial and ocular muscles, protrusion of
the tongue, opisthotonus, etc.; they usually clear up
quickly when the drug is stopped; an anti-parkinsonian
drug can be given.

Diphenoxylate Hydrochloride

Proprietary name. Lomotil (combined with small amount
of atropine sulphate).

Dose. Children: 2.5 mg 2–4 times daily.
Adults: 5 mg 3–4 times daily.

Actions and uses. It reduces excessive peristalsis in the
gastrointestinal tract. It does not have any bacterial
action. It is used to control acute and chronic diarrhoea
from a number of causes, e.g. traveller's diarrhoea,
infective diarrhoea, food poisoning, bacillary and
amoebic dysentery, etc.

Toxic and side effects. Nausea, vomiting, dizziness, restlessness and insomnia have been reported. Large single
doses can produce euphoria, and if repeated addiction.

Mebeverine

Proprietary name. Colofac.

Dose. 135 mg three times a day.

Actions and uses. It is an anti-spasmodic used in the treatment of irritable colon and other diseases of the intestinal tract.

Kaolin

Dose. 15–75 g.

Actions and uses. It is a hydrated aluminium silicate used to absorb gases or poisonous substances produced in the bowel by intestinal infections, and the treatment of diarrhoea. It is used as a dusting powder. A heavier form is used in kaolin poultices.

Ispagula Husk

Proprietary names. Fybogel, Isogel.

Dose. 1 sachet (3.5 g) or 2 teaspoonfuls twice a day after meals.

Actions and uses. The chief ingredient in this preparation is ispaghula husk. Two sachets daily provide 7 g of natural fibre with a capacity to retain 40 times its own weight of water. It is used when a high fibre content of the faeces is required, as in irritable colon syndrome and diverticulosis. The intra-colonic pressure is reduced. The bulky faeces are easily passed without straining.

Toxic and side effects. It is contra-indicated for patients with colonic atrophy, senile megacolon and intestinal obstruction. As the preparation contains sodium it should not be given to patients who are on a low sodium intake.

18 · Purgatives

The terms purgative, laxative and aperient all mean the same thing. Those in use can be classified into: (a) those that increase the bulk of the intestinal contents and so increase peristalsis (e.g. magnesium sulphate, agar); (b) those that irritate the intestine (e.g. cascara, senna). Bisacodyl acts on the muscle of the large intestine, and Beogex is given as a suppository and liberates carbon dioxide in the bowel. There are numerous preparations in which several purgatives are combined.

Magnesium Sulphate

Other name. Epsom Salts.

Dose. 5–15 g.

Actions and uses. It is a saline purge which acts by maintaining fluid in the bowel, which becomes distended, and so stimulating peristalsis. Given in the morning before breakfast and followed by a hot drink, it produces an evacuation within an hour or two. Smaller doses may be used daily to treat chronic constipation.

To stimulate the emptying of the gall-bladder 50 ml of a 25 per cent solution in water is given by mouth on an empty stomach or through a duodenal tube directly into the duodenum.

A magnesium sulphate paste may be applied to a boil or carbuncle to cause the central slough to separate off.

Sodium Sulphate

Other name. Glauber's Salt.

Dose. 5–15 g.

Actions and uses. It is a saline purge with actions and uses similar to those of magnesium sulphate.

Cascara Sagrada

Dose. Dry extract: 100–250 mg.
Liquid extract: 2–5 ml.

Actions and uses. It is a drug obtained from the bark of a shrub. Acting by stimulation of the large intestine, it produces effects within 8 to 12 hours. It is, in the ordinary doses, one of the mildest of the irritant purgatives.

Phenolphthalein

Dose. 50–300 mg.

Actions and uses. It is an irritant purgative, producing effects within 8 to 12 hours. As some of it is absorbed from the bowel and then excreted from the liver into the bile and so into the intestine again, the effect of one dose may be continued over several days. Some of it is excreted in the urine; if the urine is alkaline it gives it a red colour.

Toxic and side effects. Some people are sensitive to it and develop a skin rash. Prolonged administration can cause renal damage, and because of this and its cumulative effects, repeated taking of it is inadvisable.

Senna

Other names. Senna fruit, senna leaves.

Proprietary name. Senokot (contains the active principle of senna pod).

Dose. 500 mg–2 g.

Actions and uses. It is an irritant purgative, obtained from the pods, fruit and leaf of a plant, and usually given as an infusion. It acts in about 8 to 12 hours. It may make acid urine go yellow or brown and alkaline urine go red.

Castor Oil

Other name. Oleum ricini.

Dose. 2–5 ml.

Actions and uses. It is an oil which in the bowel becomes changed into an irritant purgative acting in 3 to 6 hours. It does not act if the patient has obstructive jaundice.

It can be instilled into an eye for a conjunctival injury. It is combined with zinc oxide in zinc and castor oil ointment.

Toxic and side effects. It can induce labour if given in large doses at the appropriate time, and has a reputation as an abortifacient.

Agar

Dose. 4 g once or twice a day.

Actions and uses. It is an extract of a seaweed that grows in the Pacific Ocean. It absorbs and retains water as it passes through the bowel, lubricating its contents and increasing their bulk. It is used in the treatment of chronic constipation. It may be combined with other purgatives, e.g. cascara, phenolphthalein.

Bisacodyl

Proprietary name. Dulcolax.

Dose. 5–10 mg by mouth; or 10 mg in suppository.

Actions and uses. It is a purgative which acts by stimulating the muscle of the large intestine. It may be given by mouth or as a suppository. It is used before operations in place of an enema, to empty the bowel before a barium enema, and to relieve constipation in old people.

Beogex

Proprietary name. Beogex.

Dose. One suppository.

Actions and uses. It is composed of chemical substances which, when the suppository is inserted into the rectum, liberate carbon dioxide. It has been recommended as a laxative before and after operations, before x-ray examination of the bowel, and for old, bed-ridden or senile patients.

19 · Vitamins

Vitamins are chemical substances that occur in many foods and are essential for many processes in the body, especially growth, the health of the skin and mucous membranes, the health of the nervous system, the normal functioning of the gastrointestinal tract, the utilization of minerals and carbohydrates, and resistance to infection. With an adequate and varied diet vitamin deficiency should not occur; but if amounts of food are inadequate – as in underprivileged countries – or when special demands have to be met – as in pregnancy and early childhood – or when a person – for one reason or another (alcoholism, drug addiction, food-faddism, mental retardation, psychosis, or senility) – does not take an adequate diet, evidence of vitamin deficiency may be observed. Vitamin B deficiency can produce beriberi and pellagra, vitamin C deficiency scurvy, and vitamin D deficiency rickets or osteomalacia. Vitamin K is necessary for blood formation. The indiscriminate use of unnecessary vitamins in various combinations for vague unspecified conditions is to be deplored.

Vitamin A

Proprietary names. Prepalin, Ro-A-Vit, Vitavel A.

Dose. Prevention.

Infants: 1 500 units daily.

Children: 4 500 units daily.

Adults: 2 500 units daily.

Pregnant and Nursing Mothers: 6 000–8 000 units daily.

Treatment.

Night blindness: 5 000–10 000 units for a few days.

Xerophthalmia: 60 000 units for a few days.

Actions and uses. Vitamin A is a fat-soluble vitamin found in fish-liver oils, butter and vitaminized margarine. It is necessary for growth and for the health of the skin, mucous membranes, eye and nervous system. Lack of it causes xerophthalmia, night-blindness and stunted growth.

Toxic and side effects. In young children overdosage can cause loss of appetite, failure to thrive, a rough skin, fever, bone thickenings, pruritus, bulging of the fontanelles of the skull, and enlargement of the liver. These conditions clear up when the administration of the vitamin is stopped.

Halibut Liver Oil

Dose. 1–3 capsules daily. (1 capsule contains about 4 500 units.)

Actions and uses. Halibut liver oil is obtained from the livers of halibut, a fish. It contains both vitamin A and vitamin D. Both these vitamins are fat-soluble and are found also in milk, butter and vitaminized margarine. Vitamin D can be formed in the skin by sunlight.

Toxic and side effects. See Vitamin A for toxic effects arising from overdosage of vitmin A, and Calciferol for toxic effects from overdosage of vitamin D.

Aneurine Hydrochloride

Other names. Vitamin B$_1$, aneurine, thiamine.

Proprietary names. Benerva, Betavel, Betaxan.

Dose. Prevention: 2–5 mg daily by mouth.
   Treatment: 25–100 mg daily by mouth or by subcutaneous or intramuscular injection.

Actions and uses. Aneurine is a member of the vitamin B
   group and is present in many foods, especially whole
   grain, yeast, and pork. The daily requirement is 1–2 mg;
   pregnant women require more. Beriberi is caused by
   lack of it and other members of the B group. It is given
   by mouth to prevent or treat beriberi. Injection is
   necessary only when it is not being absorbed from the
   bowel or when there is heart failure. Aneurine is also
   given for the treatment of neuritis of various kinds and
   when absorption of vitamin B from the bowel is
   reduced by chronic disease.

Toxic and side effects. Toxic effects are not seen except
   when large amounts (over 50 mg) are injected.

Nicotinic Acid

Other name. Niacin.

Proprietary name. Nicovel.

Dose. Prevention: 15–30 mg daily.
   Treatment: 50–250 mg daily.

Actions and uses. It is a member of the vitamin B group.
   Absence of adequate amounts of it from the diet is one
   of the factors in the production of pellagra. It – or its
   amide, nicotinamide – is given to prevent or treat
   pellagra.

Nicotinamide

Other names. Niacinamide, nicotylamide.

Proprietary name. Nicovel.

Dose. Prevention: 15–30 mg daily.
Treatment: 50–250 mg daily by mouth or intravenous injection.

Actions and uses. It is a member of the vitamin B group. Its actions are similar to those of nicotinic acid. It is used in the prevention and treatment of pellagra.

Riboflavine

Other names. Vitamin B_2, vitamin G, lactoflavin.

Proprietary names. Beflavit, Ribovel.

Dose. Prevention: 1–4 mg.
Treatment: 5–10 mg.

Actions and uses. It is a member of the vitamin B group and occurs in many foods. Lack of it causes degenerative changes in the skin, mucous membranes and eyes. Normal adult requirements are 1.5–3 mg daily. Deficiency can be prevented or cured by administration of the drug.

Pyridoxine Hydrochloride

Other names. Vitamin B_6, adermine hydrochloride.

Proprietary names. Benadon, Hexa-Betalin, Pyrivel.

Dose. For pyridoxine-dependent anaemia in adults: 50–150 mg daily in divided doses.

For vomiting in adults: 20–100 mg daily in divided doses, by mouth or injection.

For pyroxidine-dependent fits in infants: 4 mg per kilogram of body-weight for short periods.

Actions and uses. It is a member of the vitamin B group, and is present in many foods (e.g. liver, meat, yeast, cereals). Lack of it in infancy can produce irritability and fits. Lack of it in adult life can produce a hypochromic anaemia. It is also used by mouth or injection to control vomiting from various causes, e.g. radiation, post-operative, motion-sickness.

Toxic and side effects. It might have a toxic effect on a fetus, and it is not now recommended for the treatment of vomiting in pregnancy.

Ascorbic Acid

Other name. Vitamin C.

Proprietary names. Ascorvel, Redoxon.

Dose. Prevention: 25–75 mg daily.
Treatment: 200–500 mg daily.

Actions and uses. Vitamin C is essential for the development of bone and cartilage, for protection against infection, and for activities in many cells. It occurs in many fruits, vegetables and fruit-juices, and in milk. It is quickly destroyed by cooking. Lack of adequate amounts causes scurvy. It is used to prevent or treat scurvy in those liable to develop it, e.g. bottle-fed babies, underfed people, food-faddists, old people, and anyone who takes too little fresh fruit, vegetables or milk.

Alfacalcidol

Proprietary name. One-Alpha.

Dose. 1 mcg daily.

Actions and uses. This is a synthetic vitamin D preparation used in the treatment of hypoparathyroidism, osteomalacia, renal bone disease and vitamin-D dependent rickets. It can be given after parathyroidectomy to reduce the risk of hypocalcaemia.

Toxic and side effects. Excess of plasma calcium indicates that the dose is too high. Treatment is stopped and resumed in a smaller dose when the plasma calcium is normal.

Calciferol

Other name. Vitamin D_2.

Proprietary names. Sterogyl-15, Vitavel D.

Dose. Prevention of rickets: 800 units daily.
Treatment of rickets and osteomalacia: 3 000–5 000 units daily.
Treatment of hypo-parathyroidism: 50 000–20 000 units.

Actions and uses. Calciferol has actions similar to those of the naturally occurring vitamin D_3, a fat-soluble vitamin found in milk, butter, vitaminized margarine, egg-yolk and fish-liver oils. Deficiency of it causes rickets in children and osteomalacia in adults. It is used to prevent and cure both these conditions. In larger doses it is used to raise low blood calcium levels due to hypo-parathyroidism; it is used also for lupus vulgaris. It is given in relatively large doses when absorption from the bowel is poor owing to diarrhoea, steatorrhoea, or after gastrectomy and intestinal resection.

Toxic and side effects. Large doses given for a long time can produce gastrointestinal disturbances, loss of weight, headache, and the deposition of calcium in the kidneys and arteries, causing renal failure and high blood-pressure.

Phytomenadione

Other name. Vitamin K_1.

Proprietary names. Konakion, Mephyton, Aqua-Mephyton.

Dose. For haemorrhagic disease of the newly born:
   Prevention (to mother): 2.5–10 mg by mouth.
   For infant: 500 mcg–2 mg by intravenous injection.

Actions and uses. It is a vitamin essential for the clotting
   of blood. For haemorrhagic disease of the newly-born,
   it is given to the mother while she is in labour or to
   the child immediately after birth. It is given during
   labour to any mother who is being treated with any
   anti-coagulant, except heparin (against which it has no
   effect). It is also used, by mouth or intravenous injection, as an antidote to over-dosage by any anti-
   coagulant, except heparin. Bile salts must be present
   in the bowel if it is to be absorbed, and when there is
   reason to believe that they may be absent (as in obstructive jaundice) bile salts should be given with the
   phytomenadione.

Toxic and side effects. Overdosage can increase jaundice
   of the newly-born.

Acetomenaphthone

Other name. Acetomenadione.

Proprietary name. Vitavel K.

Dose. For newly-born infant: 500 mcg–2 mg.
   For adult: 5–20 mg.

Actions and uses. Similar to those of phytomenadione. It
   acts more slowly.

Menaphthone Sodium Bisulphite

Other name. Menadione sodium bisulphite.

Dose. Infants: up to 1 mg as a single dose by subcutaneous injection.

Adults: 1–2 mg daily by subcutaneous or intramuscular injection. In emergencies 10–50 mg may be injected.

Actions and uses. It is a derivative of menaphthone, which is a synthetic equivalent of vitamin K. It is used to raise the blood prothrombin level. Phytomenadione is preferred to it.

20 · Drugs for Anaemia

Drugs used to relieve anaemia are (a) preparations of iron, which are used to treat forms of microcytic anaemia in which there is a deficiency of iron; and (b) vitamin B_{12} (cyanocobalamin), a cobalt-containing vitamin used to treat pernicious anaemia and other megaloblastic anaemias.

Ferrous Sulphate

Other name. Iron sulphate.

Proprietary name. Fersolate.

Dose. Prevention: 300 mg daily.
   Treatment: 200 mg 3 times a day.

Actions and uses. Iron, in one form or another, is used in the treatment of microcytic anaemias. These anaemias result from a shortage of iron in the diet, a failure to absorb it from the intestine, blood loss, or blood destruction. Ferrous sulphate may be used for the treatment of nutritional anaemia in infancy, simple achlorhydric anaemia, simple anaemia of pregnancy, anaemia due to haemorrhage or malignant disease. In appropriate dosage it is as effective as any other oral preparation of iron.

Toxic and side effects. It can irritate the mucous membrane of the stomach, causing nausea and vomiting, and should be given after a meal. Preparations of iron make the stools black.
   Children may be poisoned by taking tablets of it, which they mistake for sweets.

Ferrous Gluconate

Proprietary names. Cerevon, Fergon, Ferronicum.

Dose. Prevention: 1000 mg daily.
   Treatment: 1.5–3 g daily in divided doses.

Actions and uses. As for ferrous sulphate.

Ferric Ammonium Citrate

Dose. Adults: 1–3 g.
    Infants: 400–800 mg.

Actions and uses. It is an iron compound, given in a
    mixture.

Toxic and side effects. It can cause diarrhoea.

Iron-Dextran Complex

Proprietary name. Imferon.

Dose. 2–5 ml (100–300 mg of elemental iron). Dose is
    calculated for each patient individually.

Actions and uses. This is a form of iron that can be given
    intramuscularly. Injections are usually given every one
    to seven days. As iron given by mouth is usually
    effective, injection is necessary only when the patient
    will not take iron by mouth, develops gastric irritation
    following an oral dose, or shows evidence of not
    absorbing iron from the bowel in sufficient amounts to
    relieve the anaemia. It may be given by slow intra-
    venous drip in anaemias of pregnancy.

Toxic and side effects. It should not be given if the patient
    is suffering from an acute infection for there is then a
    danger that he might develop an abscess at the site of
    injection. The skin over the injection-site may go brown.
    Systemic reactions and thrombophlebitis can follow
    intravenous injection.

Iron Sorbitol

Proprietary name. Jectofer.

Dose. 1.5 mg per kilo/body weight.

Actions and uses. This is a preparation of iron for intra-
    muscular injection. Injections can be given daily until
    the anaemia has been relieved. It is used when iron by
    mouth is contra-indicated (see Iron-Dextran Complex).

Cyanocobalamin

Other names. Vitamin B$_{12}$, extrinsic factor.

Proprietary names. Cobalin, Cytacon, Cytamen, Distivit B, Megalovel.

Dose. 250–1000 mcg on alternate days for 1–2 weeks.
  Maintenance dose: 1000 mcg monthly.

Actions and uses. It is a member of the vitamin B group and is essential for the formation of red blood cells. It is used in the treatment of pernicious anaemia and subacute degeneration, a disease of the spinal cord associated with pernicious anaemia. The doses given above can be doubled if the patient has subacute degeneration. It is not very effective when given by mouth.

  It is also used in the treatment of other macrocytic anaemias, in anaemia following gastrectomy, and in very big doses in neuroblastoma (a malignant tumour of sympathetic nervous tissue) in children.

Hydroxocobalamin

Proprietary names. Hydrovit, Neo-Cytamen.

Dose. 250–1000 mcg on alternate days for 1–2 weeks.
  Maintenance dose: 250 mcg once every 3–4 weeks.

Actions and uses. Similar to those of cyanobalamin. Less frequent injections are needed.

Folic Acid

Proprietary name. Folvite.

Dose. 5–20 mg daily.

Actions and uses. It is one of the vitamin B complex, and is found in meat, green vegetables, cereals and other foods. It is necessary for the formation of red blood cells, and is used in the treatment of anaemia associated with sprue, coeliac disease and idiopathic steatorrhea, and in the treatment of megaloblastic anaemias of pregnancy.

It is given in doses of 100 mcg daily to prevent folic acid type anaemia in patients taking anti-convulsants.

21 · Drugs for Diabetes Mellitus

Drugs used for diabetes mellitus fall into two groups: (a) insulin of various kinds used for severe diabetes and in diabetic emergencies, and (b) oral hypoglycaemic drugs which are given by mouth for mild cases of diabetes occurring in patients of middle age or older whose diabetes cannot be controlled by diet alone, and who still have some active islets of Langerhans which can be stimulated by these oral drugs to produce more insulin.

Insulin

Other names. Soluble insulin, ordinary insulin.

Dose. Varies with the needs of the patient.

Actions and uses. Insulin is a hormone secreted by the beta cells of the islets of Langerhans in the pancreas. It controls carbohydrate metabolism. It causes glucose to be converted into glycogen in the liver and muscles; it enables the muscles to utilize glucose fully; it is necessary for the breakdown of fat and some amino-acids. It produces a reduction of the amount of glucose in the blood (commonly called the 'blood sugar'). In diabetes mellitus there is an inadequate production of insulin, in consequence of which the blood-sugar is abnormally high and, because of the incomplete oxidation of fat, ketosis is produced.

Insulin is injected subcutaneously as a substitute for the insulin which should have been provided by the pancreas. It has no effect when taken by mouth, for it is a protein and like other proteins it is broken down by the digestive juices. The usual dose varies from 10 up to 100 units. Its actions begin in about 20 minutes, reach their maximum effect in 4 to 6 hours, and thereafter decline. This rapidly acting insulin is frequently given in combination with a more slowly acting form of insulin (such as globin zinc insulin or protamine zinc insulin) in order to maintain effective control throughout 24 hours with the minimum of injections. In emergencies (as in diabetic crisis) insulin may be injected intravenously.

Toxic and side effects. An overdose produces hypoglycaemia (too little glucose in the blood). Hypoglycaemia is characterized in the early stages by weakness, pallor, sweating, tremor, palpitations, and a sinking feeling in the stomach. With a greater degree of hypoglycaemia, confusion, fits, and unconsciousness can occur. Hypo-glycaemia is treated by giving sugar by mouth or gastric tube or glucose by intravenous injection.

Nuso (neutral soluble beef insulin) and *Actrapid* (neutral soluble pig insulin) are preparations of soluble insulin which are neutral in reaction (ordinary soluble insulin is acid). They act slightly more rapidly than ordinary soluble insulin and so are to be preferred in diabetic crisis; they are also less likely to cause discomfort at the site of injection.

Insulin Zinc Suspension

Dose. Varies with need of patient.

Actions and uses. Insulin Lente is a mixture of *Insulin Semilente* (which has a relatively quick action) and *Insulin Ultralente* (which has a slow action). Its maximum effect is produced in 10–20 hours, and as the duration of its action is about 24 hours, one daily injection is sufficient for many patients. Control of early morning blood sugar is difficult sometimes without producing too low a blood sugar in the afternoon. Control of blood sugar is unsatisfactory when the daily dose is over 60 units.

Protamine Zinc Insulin

Other name. P.Z.I.

Dose. Varies with the needs of the patient.

Actions and uses. Protamine zinc insulin is a form of insulin in which insulin is combined with a protamine and zinc chloride. Its effects are those of soluble insulin, but as it is slowly absorbed they begin later (about 4 hours after injection) and continue much longer (up to 24 hours). Soluble insulin and protamine zinc insulin are frequently given together as one injection before breakfast. The soluble insulin controls carbohydrate metabolism until the more slowly-acting protamine zinc insulin takes over. The injection has to be subcutaneous; intramuscular injection causes pain; intravenous injections of protamine zinc insulin are not given. It is not suitable for the treatment of diabetic crisis.

Toxic and side effects. Hypoglycaemia can be produced (see insulin), and, in view of the long-acting effects of protamine zinc insulin, are likely to occur at night. Allergic reactions can be produced.

Globin Zinc Insulin

Other names. Globin insulin, G.Z.I.

Dose. Varies with the needs of the patient.

Actions and uses. This is a slowly-acting form of insulin. It is not so long-acting as protamine zinc insulin. It is given subcutaneously. It is not given intravenously and is not used for the treatment of diabetic crisis.

Toxic and side effects. Hypoglycaemia can be produced. Allergic reactions are uncommon.

Chlorpropamide

Proprietary name. Diabinese.

Dose. 200–375 mg daily.

Actions and uses. It is an anti-diabetic drug given by mouth. It probably acts by stimulating the beta cells of the islets of Langerhans in the pancreas to produce more insulin, and it is effective only when there is some functioning tissue left in the pancreas to be stimulated. It is given once daily, being effective for about 24 hours. It is used for the treatment of mild diabetes only. More than 500 mg should not be given in a single dose. Control of the diabetes may not be achieved for several weeks.

Toxic and side effects. Hypoglycaemia can occur. Other side effects are nausea, vomiting, skin reactions, a reduction in the number of white cells, and jaundice. The patient should be instructed to report immediately if he has a sore throat or fever. It is contra-indicated in serious disease of the liver.

Tolbutamide

Proprietary names. Artosin, Rastinon.

Dose. 500 mg–1.5 g daily.

Actions and uses. Similar to those of chlorpropamide. It is effective for up to about 10 hours. Larger doses than those given above may be prescribed during the first 2–3 days of treatment.

Toxic and side effects. Hypoglycaemia, skin reactions and leucopenia can be produced. There is some evidence that tolbutamide and other oral anti-diabetic drugs can damage the cardio-vascular system.

Glymidine

Other name. Glycodiazine.

Proprietary names. Gondafon, Redul.

Dose. 500 mg–1.5 g daily.

Actions and uses. It is an oral anti-diabetic drug. It acts by stimulating the beta cells of the islets of Langerhans to produce more insulin, and by increasing the storage of glycogen in the liver; in animals, prolonged administration has produced an increase in the number and size of the islets. It is rapidly absorbed, achieves maximal lowering of blood-sugar in less than half an hour, and is excreted rapidly and completely. It is possibly more effective than tolbutamide. For some patients only one dose a day is necessary. It may be given in combination with insulin when insulin alone does not produce a balanced metabolic state. In pregnancy, a transfer to insulin is recommended.

Toxic and side effects. It has no serious side effects. Mild malaise and gastrointestinal upsets can occur; allergic skin reactions occur rarely. The risk of hypoglycaemia is very slight.

Glibenclamide

Proprietary names. Daonil, Euglucon.

Dose. 2.5–20 mg in a single daily dose.

Actions and uses. It is an anti-diabetic drug, of the sulphonyl-urea class, and acts by releasing insulin from the pancreas. It is a powerful drug with maximum effect in 2–4 hours. It is used for late-onset diabetes when control by other drugs is not achieved.

Toxic and side effects. It is particularly liable to cause hypoglycaemia (because of its potency) in the late morning and should be taken *during* and *not before* breakfast.

Metformin Hydrochloride

Proprietary name. Glucophage.

Dose. First 3 days: 500 mg three times a day with meals. Subsequently: up to 1000 mg three times a day with meals.

Actions and uses. It is an anti-diabetic drug given by mouth. It lowers the blood-sugar in diabetes. How it does this is uncertain; it may act by increasing the amount of glucose taken up by the tissues or by enabling any insulin in the blood to become more effective; it does not stimulate insulin secretion by the pancreas. Used alone it does not cause hypoglycaemia.

Toxic and side effects. No serious toxic or side effects are known. Gastro-intestinal upsets and a metallic taste in the mouth can be avoided by giving it with food.

Phenformin Hydrochloride

Proprietary name. Dibotin.

Dose. 25–50 mg.

Actions and uses. It is an anti-diabetic drug taken by mouth and similar in its actions and uses to metformin. It is provided in a slow-release capsule and lowers the blood-sugar for up to 12 hours.

Toxic and side effects. Rashes, depression and generalized weakness can occur. Lactic acidosis can be caused: patient is acutely ill, with dyspnoea, hyperventilation, abdominal pain, vomiting, drowsiness, coma and sometimes death. Contra-indications: severe liver disease; kidney disease severe enough to produce a blood urea of over 50 mg per 100 ml; alcoholism.

22 · Thyroid Drugs

Thyroid deficiency states (cretinism, juvenile myxoedema, myxoedema) are treated by purified thyroid hormones – thyroxine sodium and liothyronine sodium. These produce the same effects as those produced by overactivity of the thyroid gland: they increase the metabolic rate, increase the heart rate and cause loss of weight by breaking down the tissues. Precisely how they act is not known. Small doses have to be used at first because the increase in heart rate and metabolic rate puts a strain on the heart.

Thyroxine Sodium

Other names. L-thyroxine sodium, sodium laevothyroxine.

Proprietary name. Eltroxin.

Dose. Infants: 12.5 mcg daily, increased by 25 mcg every 2 weeks until effects are produced.
    Children: 50–225 mcg daily.
    Adults: 150–300 mcg daily.

Actions and uses. It is used in the treatment of cretinism, juvenile myxoedema, and myxoedema, in all of which conditions there is deficient thyroid secretion. The dose may have to be increased in cold weather and during puberty, pregnancy and lactation.

Toxic and side effects. Over-dosage can produce abdominal pain, diarrhoea, restlessness, excitement, irregular action of the heart, anginal attacks and excessive loss of weight.

Liothyronine Sodium

Other name. L-tri-iodothyronine sodium.

Proprietary name. Tertroxin.

Dose. Infants: 2.5–15 mcg daily.
Children: 15–75 mcg daily.
Adults: 50–100 mcg daily.

Actions and uses. This is the active principle of thyroid-hormone. It is given in very minute amounts, and scrupulous care must be taken in its administration. As it is rapid and powerful in its effects, it may be used to establish a diagnosis; and thereafter maintenance treatment is continued with thyroxine sodium.

Toxic and side effects. Similar to those of thyroxine sodium.

23 · Anti-thyroid Drugs

Anti-thyroid drugs are used to treat hyper-thyroidism (thyrotoxicosis) as in various ways they reduce the amount of hormones produced by the thyroid gland. They are used before operation to prepare the patient for operation or in an attempt to cure the condition, treatment by drugs for this latter purpose having to be continued for 12–18 months.

Carbimazole

Proprietary name. Neo-Mercazole.

Dose. Controlling dose: 30–60 mg daily in divided doses. Maintenance dose: 5–10 mg daily in divided doses.

Actions and uses. It has an inhibiting action on thyroid gland function as it interferes with the production of its hormones. It is used in the treatment of thyrotoxicosis and to prepare patients for thyroidectomy. Treatment is discontinued about 10 days before operation and iodine or iodides are given in order that the gland can become firm enough to be operated on. The drug has to be given cautiously if the patient is pregnant, for it passes through the placenta and can affect the fetus.

Toxic and side effects. The thyroid gland may become enlarged with an over-dosage, and the drug should therefore not be given to a patient with tracheal obstruction from a thyroid enlargement already present. Rashes, sore throat, or fever may be indications that the production of granulocytes in the blood is being interfered with; the patient should be instructed to report to the doctor at once if these occur. Swelling of joints may occur.

Potassium Perchlorate

Proprietary name. Peroidin.

Dose. 200–400 mg daily in divided doses.

Actions and uses. It prevents the thyroid gland from taking up iodine. It is occasionally used as an anti-thyroid drug in the treatment of thyrotoxicosis, usually when other anti-thyroid drugs have failed to prevent relapses or have produced side effects. Large doses may be used at first to bring the thyroid gland under control, and when signs and symptoms of hypo-thyroidism are produced the dose is reduced. Its effects being reduced by iodide, the patient should not take any cough medicine containing iodine.

Toxic and side effects. Doses larger than those given above may produce agranulocytosis or aplastic anaemia. The patient should report at once if he develops a sore throat or fever. Gastric irritation can occur.

24 · Pituitary Hormones

Pituitary hormones are obtained from the pituitary glands of animals or are synthetic equivalents.

Corticotrophin

Other names. ACTH, adreno-cortico-trophic hormone, corticotropin.

Proprietary names. Acthar, HP Acthar, Cortico-Gel, Cortrophin.

Dose. By subcutaneous or intramuscular injection (of drug labelled 'For subcutaneous or intramuscular injection'): dose varies with need of patient. It is rarely given intravenously because it can produce severe hypersensitivity reactions.

Actions and uses. It is prepared from the anterior lobe of the pituitary glands of animals. It stimulates the adrenal cortex into greater activity. For long acting effects it is combined with zinc (Corticotrophin Zinc Hydroxide) or gelatin (Corticotrophin Gelatin). Rapidly acting preparations are used in the treatment of severe allergic reactions such as status asthmaticus. Slowly acting preparations are used in rheumatoid arthritis and other chronic inflammatory conditions (see cortisone acetate). It has been used in the treatment of Bell's palsy, multiple sclerosis and drug hypersensitivity. It is also used to test the function and reserve capacity of the adrenal cortex.

Toxic and side effects. Similar to those of cortisone acetate. It is contra-indicated in peptic ulcer, severe hypertension, congestive heart failure and acute psychosis. It is given cautiously in infections, diabetes mellitus, pregnancy, peptic ulcer, moderate hypertension, and when there is a history of mental illness. The dose of insulin usually has to be increased if it is given to a diabetic patient having insulin; patients on oral hypoglycaemic drugs may require insulin. Infections are treated simultaneously with antibiotics.

Tetracosactrin

Proprietary name. Synacthen.

Dose. 250 mcg by injection or infusion.

Actions and uses. It is a synthetic corticotrophin; it does not cause allergic reactions. It is used in the treatment of status asthmaticus, drug-sensitivity reactions and anaphylactic shock, and as a test of the function of the cortex of the adrenal gland.

Oxytocin

See Section 30.

25 · Cortico-steroids

Cortico-steroids are hormones produced by the adrenal glands or similar synthetic substances. They are used when the adrenals are destroyed by disease or removed by operation, and for a number of inflammatory and degenerative conditions. The adrenal steroids have a number of actions on carbohydrate, fat, and protein metabolism, on sodium and water metabolism, and on inflammatory reactions to infection. As well, therefore, as being used when there is known adrenal insufficiency, cortico-steroids are used in a number of conditions in which they have been shown to produce beneficial effects. These conditions include rheumatoid arthritis, acute rheumatic fever, bronchial asthma, nephrosis, pemphigus, acute disseminated lupus erythematosus, poly-arteritis nodosa, acquired haemolytic anaemia, severe ulcerative colitis and several inflammatory diseases of the eye.

Cortico-steroids can interfere with the body's defence mechanisms, interfere with healing processes, and cause sodium retention and a rise in blood pressure. They should not be given in pregnancy unless there is good reason for they are thought to cause fetal abnormalities.

Patients taking steroids should carry a card saying so.

Withdrawal of adrenal cortico-steroids after prolonged administration can cause adrenal insufficiency – with weakness, nausea, loss of appetite, joint pains, fall of BP, desquamation of skin, dyspnoea, low blood sugar and sometimes death.

Cortisone Acetate

Proprietary names. Cortelan, Cortistab, Cortisyl.

Dose. 5–400 mg daily in divided doses by mouth or intramuscular injection.

12.5–50 mg daily in Addison's disease, after adrenalectomy and in pan-hypopituitarism.

Actions and uses. It is a steroid used when there is insufficient production of normal steroids from the adrenal glands or when the adrenal glands are diseased or have been removed by operation. It is frequently given in combination with the appropriate anti-infective drug.

Toxic and side effects. A peptic ulcer may be produced, or a haemorrhage or perforation from one may occur. Other complications are water retention, obesity, hypertension, diabetes, and osteoporosis. Cushing's syndrome can occur (obesity, roundness of the face, excessive hair growth, acne, and striae over the hips and shoulders). Sudden withdrawal of the drug may produce adrenal exhaustion, death, or a grave deterioration of the original condition.

Hydrocortisone Acetate

Proprietary names. Cortril, Efcortelan, Hydro-Adreson, Hydrocortistab, Hydrocortisyl, Hydrocortone.

Dose. For injection into joints: 5–50 mg.
For intravenous injection: 100 mg.

Actions and uses. It is a steroid which can be injected directly into joints in the treatment of rheumatoid arthritis and osteo-arthritis. It is given by slow intravenous infusion in the treatment of Addisonian crises or post-adrenalectomy crises. It can be used in status asthmaticus and anaphylactic shock. It is given (in combination with an antibiotic such as neomycin) in eye-drops or ointments for the treatment of inflammatory conditions of the eyes. It is given as a lotion, cream or ointment to the skin for the treatment of inflammatory conditions, itching, pruritus ani and haemorrhoids.

Hydrocortisone sodium succinate, a similar preparation, is used in lozenge form to treat ulceration of the mouth.

Toxic and side effects. Used by itself in the treatment of local inflammatory conditions it may hide the development of an infection, and it should therefore be combined with an appropriate antibiotic.

Fludrocortisone Acetate

Proprietary name. Florinef.

Dose. 1–2 mg daily.
Maintenance dose: 100–200 mcg daily.

Actions and uses. It acts like cortisone and is a powerful retainer of salt and water in the body. It is used in the treatment of Addison's disease and after adrenalectomy. The larger dose (1–2 mg) given above is used to treat Addisonian crises. It is also used in lotions or creams to treat inflammatory and itching skin disorders.

Toxic and side effects. Similar to cortisone acetate.

Dexamethasone

Proprietary names. Decadron, Dexacortisyl, Oradexon.

Dose. 500 mcg–10 mg daily in divided doses.

Actions and uses. It is a synthetic cortico-steroid with actions and uses similar to those of cortisone acetate. It is also used for the treatment of closed head trauma and cerebral oedema.

Toxic and side effects. Similar to those of cortisone acetate. It is contra-indicated in peptic ulcer, osteoporosis, thrombophlebitis, pulmonary tuberculosis, and in patients who have had mental illnesses.

Betamethasone

Proprietary names. Betnelan, Betnesol.

Dose. 500 mcg–1.0 mg by mouth; or 1.0 mg by intra-articular injection.

Actions and uses. It is similar in its actions and uses to dexamethasone. It can be injected intra-articularly for rheumatoid arthritis and osteo-arthritis. It is applied locally for eczema.

Toxic and side effcts. Similar to those of cortisone acetate. It is not injected into joints when the arthritis is due to tuberculosis or gonorrhoea.

Prednisolone

Other name. Delta-hydrocortisone

Proprietary names. Codelcortone, Delta-Cortef, Delta-cortril, Delta-Genacort, Deltastab, Precortisyl, Prednelan, Predsol.

Dose. 10–100 mg daily in divided doses.

Actions and uses. It is used in the treatment of connective tissue diseases, systemic lupus erythematosus, sarcoidosis and acute leukaemia. Intra-articular injections (of 25–50 mg) can be given in rheumatoid arthritis and osteo-arthritis. It can be given in appropriate preparations for the treatment of inflammatory conditions of the eye and skin. In the treatment of ulcerative colitis, it may be given by mouth (in doses of 10 mg, 6-hourly) at the same time as water-soluble cortico-steroids are given by rectal drip.

Toxic and side effects. Similar to those of cortisone acetate.

Methyl-prednisolone

Proprietary names. Medrone, Metastab.

Dose. 12–20 mg daily.

Actions and uses. It is a synthetic cortico-steroid. Its actions and uses are similar to prednisone, but it is effective in smaller doses.

Toxic and side effects. Similar to those of cortisone acetate.

Triamcinolone

Proprietary names. Adcortyl, Ledercort.

Dose. 8–20 mg daily in divided doses.

Actions and uses. It is similar in its actions and uses to cortisone acetate, but as it does not retain sodium in the body it is not used in Addison's disease or after adrenalectomy. It is applied locally for eczema.

Toxic and side effects. Similar to those of cortisone acetate, but (as it does not retain sodium) obesity and oedema do not occur.

26 · Female Sex Hormones

Oestrogens are used to relieve unpleasant symptoms during the menopause, to stop the production of milk from the breasts, and to treat atrophic vulvitis and kraurosis of the vulva. When they are given during the first half of the menstrual cycle they inhibit ovulation and are thus a constituent of contraceptive pills. They may be given to check bleeding in metropathia haemorrhagica and check the progress of an inoperable carcinoma of the breast. They are given, in high doses, to men to check the growth of a cancer of the prostate gland and of secondary deposits in bone.

Progesterone, the hormone of the luteal body of the ovary, and synthetic comparable drugs are used in the treatment of uterine haemorrhage and abortion. Progestogens given in pregnancy can cause masculinization of a female fetus.

Oestradiol

Other name. Estradiol.

Proprietary names. Oestroform, Ovocyclin.

Dose. 1–10 mg daily.

Actions and uses. Oestradiol is a naturally occurring oestrogen. It is used for all the purposes described above (Female Sex Hormones). It may be given by mouth, intramuscular injection, and subcutaneous implantation, in an ointment, in a pessary or in a suppository. The dose by mouth has to be five to ten times greater than that by intramuscular injection. *Oestradiol benzoate* (dose: 1–5 mg at intervals of 1 to 14 days) is a suitable preparation for intramuscular injection as it forms a deposit from which oestradiol is released gradually over several days.

Toxic and side effects. An excessive growth of the uterine mucosa can occur, and bleeding from the uterus when the drug is withdrawn.

Ethinyl-oestradiol

Proprietary names. Estigyn, Lynoral.

Dose. For the menopause: 10–50 mcg daily.
   For suppression of lactation: 100 mcg three times a day for 3 days and subsequently once daily for 6 days.

Actions and uses. This is a powerful synthetic oestrogen, used for all the purposes described above.

Toxic and side effects. Nausea, vomiting, headache and giddiness can occur.

Stilboestrol

Proprietary name. Delliposoids D.13.

Dose. For menopausal symptoms: 100 mcg–1 mg daily.
   For suppression of lactation: 5 mg three times a day for 3 days and then once a day for 6 days.
   For carcinoma of the prostate gland: 3–15 mg.

Actions and uses. It is a synthetic oestrogen used for the purposes described above.
   The normal prostate gland is hormone dependent, and giving stilboestrol can for a time check the growth of a prostatic cancer and any secondaries that may have developed.

Toxic and side effects. Nausea and vomiting can occur.

Dienoestrol

Other names. Dehydro-stilboestrol.

Dose. For the menopause: 500 mcg–5 mg daily.
   For suppression of lactation: 15 mg three times a day and subsequently once daily for 6 days.
   For carcinoma of the prostate gland: 15–30 mg daily.

Actions and uses. It is a synthetic oestrogen given by mouth, for all the purposes described above (Female Sex Hormones).

Toxic and side effects. Nausea and vomiting can occur.

Progesterone

Other names. Progestin, luteal hormone.

Proprietary name. Lutocylin-M.

Dose. 20–60 mg daily by intramuscular injection or implantation.

Actions and uses. It is the hormone secreted by the corpus luteum. It is used to treat functional uterine bleeding, threatened abortion, and habitual abortion, but it is of doubtful value in the prevention of abortion.

Ethisterone

Proprietary name. Lutocyclin.

Dose. 25–100 mg daily.

Actions and uses. Its actions and uses are similar to those of progesterone. It acts when given by mouth (the tablet to be placed under the tongue). It can be given by implantation.

Norethisterone

Proprietary names. Norlutin-A, Primolut-N.

Dose. 5–15 mg daily.

Actions and uses. Its actions and uses are those of progesterone. It can be given by mouth. Given in the 2nd half of the menstrual cycle, it may prevent premenstrual tension.

Chlorotrianisene

Proprietary name. Tace.

Dose. 12–48 mg daily.

Actions and uses. It is a synthetic oestrogen used to treat menopausal symptoms and to suppress lactation, and in men to treat cancer of the prostate gland.

Toxic and side effects. Nausea and vomiting can occur. Withdrawal bleeding can occur. The dry dust should not come into contact with the skin nor be inhaled, and anyone handling the dust should wear a mask and rubber gloves.

Quinestradol

Proprietary name. Pentovis.

Dose. 250 mcg twice a day for 14 days.

Actions and uses. It is an oestrogen given by mouth for the treatment of senile vaginitis, kraurosis vulvae, and in the pre-operative treatment of post-menopausal women before gynaecological operations. Treatment may have to be continued for a further 14 days.

27 · Male Sex Hormones

Testosterone Propionate

Proprietary names. Neo-Hombreol, Testaform, Testoral.

Dose. 5–25 mg once or twice weekly by intramuscular injection; or 400 mg by pellet implanted subcutaneously every 6 months.

Actions and uses. Testosterone is the male sex hormone (or androgen). It is formed in cells in the testis and is responsible for the development and maintenance of the male sex organs and male secondary sexual characteristics. Testosterone propionate is given, by intramuscular injection or implanted pellets, to promote sexual development in men in cases of eunuchoidism, after castration, or when sexual characteristics have not developed. It is given to women to suppress lactation, to treat some forms of periodic uterine bleeding, to relieve mastodynia, and (in doses of 100–300 mg weekly) to relieve inoperable cancer of the breast and secondary deposits especially in bone. It may be given in combination with oestrogens to relieve menopausal symptoms. It is inactive when given by mouth.

Toxic and side effects. Virilism (masculine features appearing in a woman) can be produced by large doses. Oedema and hyper-calcaemia can occur.

Methyl Testosterone

Proprietary names. Glosso-Sterandryl, Perandren.

Dose. Men: 25–50 mg daily.
Women: 5–20 mg daily.

Actions and uses. Its actions and uses are similar to those of testosterone propionate. It can be given by mouth. For the treatment of inoperable cancer of the breast large doses of the drug (50–100 mg daily) are required.

Toxic and side effects. It can produce virilism in women if given in large doses. Obstructive jaundice can occur.

Fluoxymesterone

Proprietary name. Ultandren.

Dose. 1–20 mg daily.

Actions and uses. Similar to those of testosterone propionate. It is given by mouth.

Toxic and side effects. Similar to those of testosterone propionate.

Cyproterone Acetate

Proprietary name. Androcur.

Dose. 50–100 mg twice a day.

Actions and uses. It is a synthetic steroid hormone which as it reduces sexual drive in the male is used to treat male hypersexuality and sexual deviation. The patient should be willing to try to diminish his unacceptable sexual urges and should give written consent to the treatment, which has to be continued indefinitely.

Toxic and side effects. Impaired testicular function with inhibition of sperm function can occur, and so can fatigue, enlargement of the breasts, and fluctuation of weight. It is thought that these effects are reversible. The drug is contra-indicated if there is a history of thrombosis or embolism, and if the patient has an acute impairment of liver function.

28 · Oral Contraceptives

Most oral contraceptives taken in Britain are composed of two synthetic steroid hormones, an oestrogen and a progestogen. They act by preventing the ovaries from releasing an ovum, by stopping the endometrium from developing into the state necessary to receive a fertilized ovum, and by causing the mucus of the cervix of the uterus to become so thick and tough that spermatozoa cannot penetrate it.

Oral contraceptives consist of (a) a progestogen, (b) ethinyloestradiol or mestranol. There is also a progesterone-only type taken every day. Many preparations are available. They vary in the proportion of each steroid in them and in containing steroids of different strengths. To be effective they have to be taken strictly in accordance with the manufacturer's instructions. These usually state that one tablet has to be taken daily for 21 days, starting on the 5th day, the 1st day of bleeding being the 1st day, followed by a 7 day interval. Three or 4 days after the completion of a course the woman has 'withdrawal bleeding'.

The best 'pill' for any woman is the one that:
a has the smallest effective dose of oestrogen – it should not be more than 50 mcg;
b produces the fewest undesirable side effects;
c produces the most advantageous side effects.

Undesirable side effects
venous thrombosis – rare with pills containing 50 mcg
or less of oestrogen
hypertension
fluid retention
breast discomfort
greasy skin
hirsutism
fungus infections
premenstrual tension
gain of weight
mucous vaginal discharge

acne
dryness of vagina

Contra-indications
a history of venous thrombosis
atrial fibrillation or other condition in which arterial
 embolism can occur
some cancers of the breast

Advantageous side effects
relief of premenstrual tension
relief of dysmenorrhoea
less acne
less iron-deficiency anaemia

29 · Diuretics

Diuretics are drugs used to reduce oedema by increasing the amount of urine excreted.

Most diuretics act by causing the retention of sodium in the renal tubules and so retaining the fluid in which the sodium is dissolved. With a diminution of renal tubular absorption much more urine is passed. Some diuretics cause an excessive amount of potassium to be excreted as well, and to compensate for this some preparations have potassium chloride added, being distinguished by the letter 'K' after their name, e.g. Esidrex-K, Hydrosaluric-K. Some other diuretics, such as spironolactone, retain potassium and are to be preferred as some patients cannot tolerate potassium supplements.

These drugs are contra-indicated in acute and advanced nephritis. Plasma electrolyte levels should be measured regularly. An excessive use of a diuretic can cause severe disturbance of the electrolyte and acid-base balance of the body. Diuretics have to be given cautiously when there is a likelihood that the patient has an enlarged prostate gland or a stricture of the urethra.

Acetazolamide

Proprietary name. Diamox.

Dose. 250–500 mg on alternate days.

Actions and uses. It acts on the kidney by stopping the action of an enzyme called carbonic anhydrase; by this action, more sodium and therefore more water is excreted. The drug is a fairly weak diuretic, and owing to various biochemical changes it produces it is not continuously effective if it is given continuously. It is therefore given on alternate days.

It is also used to reduce intra-ocular tension in glaucoma.

Toxic and side effects. Drowsiness or tingling in the limbs are an indication that the drug should be reduced in dosage or stopped. It should be stopped if renal damage occurs or the number of granulocytes or platelets in the blood is reduced below normal.

Xipamide

Proprietary name. Diurexan.

Dose. 20–40 mg daily.

Actions and uses. It is a diuretic used to relieve oedema. Diuresis lasts for up to 12 hours. Compared with frusemide, its action is gradual. The BP is lowered.

Toxic and side effects. Similar to those of other diuretics.

Chlorothiazide

Proprietary name. Saluric.

Dose. 200 mg–2 g daily for 4–5 days and then on alternate days.

Actions and uses. It is a non-mercurial diuretic which acts by stopping the absorption of electrolytes by the renal tubules and thereby compelling the excretion of more water. After daily administration for 4–5 days, it is given on alternate days or twice a week. If the oedema is very resistant to treatment, chlorothiazide and mersalyl may be given together. If treatment is given for a long time, excessive amounts of potassium are excreted; to maintain an adequate amount of potassium in the body-tissues and fluids potassium salts (chloride, citrate or gluconate) are given on days when the drug is not given; apricots, oranges or plums (which contain potassium) may be helpfully included in the diet.

Chlorothiazide is used in the treatment of oedema, premenstrual oedema, toxaemia of pregnancy and, with hypotensive drugs (which it potentiates) in the treatment of hypertension.

Toxic and side effects. It has to be used with care when there is any impairment of renal or hepatic function. It can cause hepatic coma if hepatic function is impaired. Nausea and epigastric pain can occur. Allergic phenomena can occur. An attack of gout may be precipitated in a gouty person. A reduction of granulocytes or platelets below normal levels occurs rarely. The dose of a ganglion-blocking drug used in the treatment of hypertension should be halved if a thiazide is given. Purpura and acute pancreatitis have occurred. Diabetes may be aroused in a latent diabetic.

Hydrochlorothiazide

Proprietary names. Direma, Esidrex, Hydrosaluric.

Dose. 25–50 mg.

Actions and uses. It is used as a diuretic and for the treatment of hypertension. It is similar in its actions and uses to chlorothiazide. The excretion of potassium is less.

Toxic and side effects. Similar to those of chlorothiazide.

Hydroflumethiazide

Proprietary names. Hydrenox, Naclex.

Dose. 25–100 mg daily or on alternate days.

Actions and uses. It is used as a diuretic and for the treatment of hypertension. It is similar in its actions to chlorothiazide.

Toxic and side effects. Similar to those of chlorothiazide.

Bendrofluazide

Proprietary names. Aprinox, Centyl, Neo-Naclex.

Dose. 2.5–10 mg daily or on alternate days.

Actions and uses. Similar to those of chlorothiazide.

Toxic and side effects. Similar to chlorothiazide.

Frusemide

Proprietary name. Lasix.

Dose. 40–200 mg by mouth daily; or 20–60 mg intramuscularly or intravenously.

Actions and uses. It is a powerful and safe diuretic used in the treatment of oedema due to congestive heart failure or cirrhosis of the liver. It can be given intravenously when rapid action is required, as in acute pulmonary oedema.

Toxic and side effects. If a lot of urine is excreted, the amount of potassium in the body may fall to an undesirably low level, and the diet should be supplemented by potassium given by mouth. Some patients complain of dryness of the mouth. A rapid but reversible deafness can occur, due to toxic effects on the inner ear.

Triameterene

Proprietary name. Dytac.

Dose. 50–100 mg twice a day.

Actions and uses. It is an oral diuretic, acting on the distal part of the renal tubule only. It begins to be effective in about 30 minutes, produces its maximum effect between 2 and 6 hours, and is eliminated almost completely within 24 hours. It is used to treat oedema due to heart failure, to the nephrotic syndrome, or to cirrhosis of the liver. Potassium is retained, and therefore potassium supplements are not necessary.

Toxic and side effects. It may produce nausea and vomiting. Excess excretion of urine causes hypotension, headache, giddiness, and increased blood-urea, and excessive electrolyte loss.

Amiloride

Proprietary name. Midamor.

Dose. 5–20 mg daily.

Actions and uses. It is a more powerful diuretic than triameterene, but acts in the same way. Potassium is retained and therefore potassium supplements are not necessary.

Toxic and side effects. As for triameterene.

Chlorthalidone

Proprietary name. Hygroton.

Dose. Initial: 100–200 mg 3 times a week.
  Maintenance: 100–200 mg twice a week.

Actions and uses. It is a diuretic used to treat oedema due to congestive heart failure, nephrotic syndrome and cirrhosis of the liver. It is also used to treat premenstrual tension and to prevent and treat late toxaemia of pregnancy. It starts to act in 1–2 hours and its effects last for 48–72 hours. Potassium supplements are required when the serum potassium is low.

Toxic and side effects. Nausea can occur. Diabetes can be made worse or latent diabetes precipitated into frank diabetes; during prolonged treatment, blood-sugar estimations should be made from time to time and the urine examined for sugar.

Quinethazone

Proprietary name. Aquamox.

Dose. 50–100 mg in a single daily dose.

Actions and uses. It is an oral diuretic, believed to act on the renal tubules. It is used, either alone or in combination with acetazolamide, in the treatment of oedema due to chronic heart failure.

Toxic and side effects. Prolonged daily administration may produce an excessive excretion of potassium and an increase in the blood-urea.

Bumetanide

Proprietary name. Burinex.

Dose. 1–4 mg daily.
   500 mcg–1.0 mg by intravenous or intramuscular injection.

Actions and uses. It is a powerful diuretic with a rapid onset and short duration of action, diuresis beginning in 30 minutes and lasting for 4–6 hours. It is used for the treatment of oedema due to heart failure, cirrhosis of the liver and kidney disease. It is given by injection in the treatment of pulmonary oedema. It is not used in the treatment of hypertension.

Toxic and side effects. It can produce electrolyte disturbance and disturbance of hearing. It is not recommended for children and in pregnancy. Muscle pain can occur in patients with renal failure on high doses.

Spironolactone

Proprietary name. Aldactone-A.

Dose. 25–200 mg daily in divided doses.

Actions and uses. It is a synthetic steroid which increases the excretion of chloride and water by the kidney. It is used as a diuretic, in combination with another diuretic, e.g. chlorothiazine or mersalyl. Its full effect may not be seen for 3–4 days. Potassium is retained, and potassium supplements are not necessary.

Toxic and side effects. Uraemia or hepatic coma can develop if too much urine is excreted. It is given cautiously to patients with renal insufficiency. Gynaecomastia (enlargement of male breast) can occur.

Potassium Citrate

Dose. 1–4 g.

Actions and uses. It makes the urine less acid. It is used
in the treatment of inflammations of the bladder, to
provide potassium for the body when chlorothiazide
and other diuretics are over-stimulating its excretion,
and to prevent the formation of crystals in the kidney
when sulphonamides are being given.

Sodium Citrate

Dose. 1–4 g.

Actions and uses. Its actions and uses are similar to those
of potassium citrate. It may be added to milk to
prevent the formation of large curds; for infant feeding,
125 mg in 5 ml of water is added to each feed.

It can be used in a 3 per cent solution to wash out
the bladder. The same strength of solution is used to
prevent the clotting of blood in glassware and syringes.

30 · Drugs used in Obstetrics and Gynaecology

The drugs used in midwifery are (a) those used to reduce pain (e.g. pethidine), (b) anaesthetics (e.g. gas and oxygen, trilene), (c) tranquillizers, (d) hypnotics, and (e) drugs such as oxytocin and ergometrine used to stimulate contractions of the muscle of the uterus.

The drugs used in gynaecology include (a) hormones and (b) drugs used to treat infections.

Oxytocin

Proprietary names. Pitocin, Syntocinon.

Dose. 1–5 units by injection.

Actions and uses. The oxytocic principle of the posterior lobe of the pituitary gland is used to induce labour, to overcome uterine inertia, and to stop haemorrhage after child-birth. To induce labour or overcome uterine inertia it is given in a drip of 1 litre of 5 per cent dextrose solution by slow intravenous infusion. To stop haemorrhage it is given by intramuscular, subcutaneous or slow intravenous infusion.

Tablets of oxytocin are sometimes given to induce labour but are less satisfactory than intravenous infusion.

Toxic and side effects. Wrongly used, it can cause rupture of the uterus and tearing of soft tissues. It is contra-indicated if the baby's head is too big for the mother's pelvis, in placenta praevia, and if the fetus is distressed.

Ergometrine Maleate

Other name. Ergometrine.

Dose. 500 mcg–1 mg by mouth; 200 mcg–1.0 mg by intramuscular injection; or 100–500 mcg by intravenous injection.

Actions and uses. It increases the tone and stimulates rhythmic contractions of the muscle of the uterus. It acts in about 1 minute when injected intravenously, in about 2 minutes when injected intramuscularly, and in about 8 minutes when taken by mouth. It is used to prevent and treat haemorrhage after child-birth.

Toxic and side effects. Nausea and vomiting can occur.

Syntometrine

Proprietary name. Syntometrine.

Dose. 1 ml intramuscularly.

Actions and uses. It contains in 1 ml ergometrine maleate 500 mcg and oxytocin 5 units. Given in child-birth after the delivery of the baby's shoulders, it is used to prevent post-partum haemorrhage.

Dinoprostone

Dose.
    (a) For termination of pregnancy: 2 mg extra-amniotically; 5 mg intravenously;
    (b) For induction of labour: a smaller intravenous dose.

Actions and uses. It is a prostaglandin which stimulates contractions of the uterine muscle. Special solutions and infusion techniques are necessary.

Toxic and side effects. Nausea, vomiting, diarrhoea, headache and vasodilatation can occur, but are not serious.

Metronidazole

Proprietary name. Flagyl.

Dose. 200 mg three times a day for 7 days.

Actions and uses. It is given by *mouth* in the treatment of
Trichomonas vaginalis of the genitourinary tract in both
women and men. A second course may be given. It
appears to be safe to use during pregnancy. As the
infection is spread by sexual intercourse, it may be
necessary to treat sexual partners at the same time.

It can be used to treat gingivitis (infection of the
gums) in patients with a trichomonal infection there.
It is used in the treatment of giardiasis and amoebic
dysentery.

It is given (in doses of 200–700 mg three times a
day) to kill anaerobic organisms after operation on the
lower bowel or pelvic organs.

Toxic and side effects. Gastrointestinal disturbances,
headache, dizziness and a feeling of constriction in the
chest have been reported. Patients on the drug should
not take alcohol as it can cause an acute confusional
state.

Nimorazole

Proprietary names. Naxogin, Nulogyl.

Dose. 250 mg twice daily for 6 days.

Actions and uses. It acts like metronidazole, but is more
quickly absorbed.

Clotrimazole

Proprietary name. Canesten.

Dose. 1 tablet placed high in the vagina every night for 6 consecutive nights.

Actions and uses. It is used in the treatment of trichomonal and *candida* infections of the vagina. If necessary treatment can be continued for up to 18 consecutive nights. A cream is available for simultaneous application to the vulva and for the treatment of the sexual partner of the affected woman.

The same cream is used in the treatment of fungus infections of the skin, being applied 2–3 times a day; its application has to be continued for at least 2 weeks after apparent recovery.

Toxic and side effects. None.

Nystatin

Proprietary name. Nystatin.

Dose. 100 000 units (1 tablet) intravaginally.

Actions and uses. It is an antibiotic used in the treatment of fungal infections. It is used locally, by the insertion of 1–2 tablets daily into the vagina, for the treatment of *Monilia* infections.

Isoxsuprine Hydrochloride

Proprietary name. Duvadilan.

Dose. 20 mg three times a day.

Actions and uses. It relaxes the muscle of the uterus and is given by mouth to relieve the pain of severe primary dysmenorrhoea, treatment being begun two days before a period is due. Given intravenously it is sometimes used to stop premature labour. It is also used as a vaso-dilator in peripheral and cerebral vascular disease.

Toxic and side effects. Given intravenously it can cause a serious fall in blood-pressure.

Clomiphene

Proprietary name. Clomid.

Dose. 50 mg daily for 5 days from day 7 to day 12 of menstrual cycle.

Actions and uses. It is a 'fertility drug', used to induce ovulation by stimulating the production of follicular-stimulating hormone by the pituitary gland. The dose is regulated in accordance with estimations of the amount of hormones in the urine.

Side effect. Multiple pregnancy.

31 · Drugs for the Skin

Drugs used for the diseases of the skin are usually applied 'topically', i.e. to the affected areas. For general diseases some drugs may be given by mouth either to relieve the local condition or to improve the natural and other other resistances of the body.

Lotions

Lotions are watery solutions used for inflamed, weeping or eczematous areas of skin. They relieve irritation, cool the skin, check inflammation, and remove crusts and debris.

Aluminium acetate lotion contains 5 per cent of aluminium acetate. It is used for its cooling and astringent actions.

Calamine lotion contains calamine (which is zinc carbonate coloured with ferric chloride), zinc oxide and phenol. It is used for inflamed and irritating areas. An *oily calamine lotion* is available.

Eau d'Alibour is a copper-zinc lotion containing copper sulphate, zinc sulphate and camphor. It is an antiseptic and astringent used for impetigo, intertrigo and minor skin infections.

Lead lotion contains 2 per cent of strong lead subacetate solution. It is used mainly for its cooling property.

Compound lead lotion contains strong lead acetate solution 2 per cent with starch, zinc oxide and glycerin.

Mercuric and resorcin lotion contains mercuric chloride, resorcin, salicylic acid, and 50 per cent of industrial methylated spirit. It is used for seborrheic dermatitis and pityriasis capitis.

Potassium permanganate solution contains 0.1 per cent of potassium permanganate and has to be further diluted 1 part in 7 of water. It is an antiseptic. The *strong solution* contains 4 per cent of potassium permanganate and has to be further diluted 1 teaspoonful to 1 pint of water.

Tar and tannic acid lotion is a solution of coal tar and

tannic acid. It is used for weeping eczema and pompholyx. Mercuric chloride may be added to it if the lesion is infected.

Ointments

Ointments are preparations in which the active ingredient, which may be a solid or liquid, is incorporated in a greasy base. Some bases (such as lanoline) are absorbed by the skin, others (such as paraffin) are not. When an ointment is smeared lightly on the skin, some of the active ingredient exerts a superficial action on the surface of the skin; when an ointment is rubbed on the skin, some enters the sweat glands and hair follicles and more of the active ingredient is absorbed.

Calamine Ointment consists of 16 per cent of calamine (which is zinc carbonate coloured with ferric chloride) in white soft paraffin. It is used to soothe inflamed, itching lesions.

Calamine and Coal Tar Ointment consists of calamine, zinc oxide and coal tar solution in white soft paraffin. It is used for inflamed and eczematous lesions.

Menthol and Eucalyptus Ointment contains menthol 1 per cent and eucalyptus oil 4 per cent. It is used to treat chilblains.

Sulphur Ointment contains sublimed sulphur .It is used in the treatment of scabies. It can cause dermatitis.

White Precipitate Ointment contains 2.5 per cent of ammoniated mercury and is used for ringworm infections and ulcerative impetigo.

Whitfield's Ointment contains benzoic acid and salicylic acid. It is used for fungus (ringworm) infections of the toes and groin.

Zinc Ointment contains 15 per cent of zinc oxide. It is used for mildly inflamed areas of skin.

Zinc and Castor Oil Ointment contains zinc oxide and castor oil. It is used to prevent bedsores.

Zinc and Coal Tar Paste (White's tar paste) contains zinc oxide, coal tar and starch. It is used for psoriasis and chronic eczema. Coal tar can produce photosensitivity to natural or artificial sunlight.

Creams

Creams consist of emulsifying agents, water, and active ingredient, such as calamine. The emulsifying agents aid the absorption of the active ingredient, and the evaporation of water from the cream produces a cooling effect.

Compound Calamine Cream contains calamine, zinc oxide and zinc stearate. For itching lesions, coal tar or phenol may be added.

Coal Tar Cream contains solution of coal tar and liquid paraffin. It is used for eczema.

Zinc Oxide Cream contains zinc oxide. For infected lesions ichthammol 2 per cent (which is a mild antiseptic) may be added.

Dithranol creams (*Proprietary preparations*: Dithocream, Psoradate) are used for chronic discoid psoriasis.

Poultices

Poultices are used to soften and remove crusts.

Starch poultice contains powdered starch and boric acid in water.

Cortico-Steroids

Cortico-steroids are applied to the skin (in sprays, lotions, creams or ointments) to check inflammation and relieve itching. *Hydrocortisone* is the one most commonly used. There are numerous proprietary preparations in which a cortico-steroid is combined with an antibiotic or other anti-infective drug. When treatment is prolonged some cortico-steroid may be absorbed by the body.

Fungicides

Fungus infections of the skin, hair, nails and mucous membranes are treated by local applications or, some of them, by drugs given by mouth.

Zinc Undecenoate Ointment contains zinc undecenoate and undecenoic acid. A dusting powder is available.

Benzoic Acid Compound Ointment (Whitfield's Ointment) contains benzoic acid and salicyclic acid.

Magenta Paint (Castellani's Paint) contains magenta and phenol.

Tolnaftate (Proprietary Name: Tinaderm) is an anti-fungicide active against the common skin fungi that cause tinea infections.

Griseofulvin

Proprietary name. Grisovin.

Dose. 500 mg–1 g daily by mouth.

Actions and uses. It is an antibiotic which, given by mouth, is absorbed into the skin, hair and nails, acting there as an anti-fungal agent. It is used in the treatment of tinea (ringworm) of the skin, nails and hair. Treatment for tinea of the nails has to be continued for weeks or months. It is best absorbed after fatty food.

Toxic and side effects. Gastrointestinal disturbances and headache can occur. Rarely, a reduction of the number of granulocyte cells of the blood occurs.

Anti-Parasitic Preparations

Anti-parastic preparations are used in the treatment of scabies, pediculosis, and insect bites.

Benzyl Benzoate Application contains benzyl benzoate 25 per cent. To treat scabies the whole body (except the head and neck) is painted all over on two successive days. This treatment has largely replaced treatment by sulphur ointment, which is less effective and can cause dermatitis.

Malathion (Proprietary name: Prioderm) is used to kill head-lice. The lotion is sprinkled on the scalp and rubbed; care must be taken that none gets into the eyes. The lotion is allowed to dry and the hair is untouched for 12 hours; it is then shampooed and the dead lice and nits removed by fine-combing while wet. The lotion is inflammable and toxic; it should be applied only by nurses and health visitors; gloves should be worn while it is being applied.

Dicophane (DDT) Dusting Powder is used to kill pediculi and insects.

Gamma Benzene Hydrochloride is rubbed into the hair to kill pediculi. The hair must not be washed for 24 hours. If taken by mouth, it can cause fits.

Dimethyl Phthalate (DMP) is an insect repellant, effective against fleas, mosquitoes, midges and other insects. It is effective for several hours after application. It is applied as a lotion or cream. It should not be applied near the eyes or mucous membranes.

Pastes

A paste consists of a greasy base in which powder is suspended in amounts sufficient to make the whole preparation semi-solid. Pastes absorb secretions, allow evaporation of moisture, and are used where there is exudation and crusting, particularly in flexures of the skin.

Aluminium Compound Paste contains aluminium powder, zinc oxide and liquid paraffin. It is used to protect the skin around colostomies and open wounds.

Coal Tar Paste contains coal tar, zinc oxide and starch. It is used for eczema, dermatitis and lichen simplex.

Compound Zinc Paste contains zinc oxide and starch. It is used to protect inflamed areas.

Magnesium Sulphate Paste (Morison's paste) contains magnesium sulphate 39 per cent and phenol 0.5 per cent in glycerin. It is hypertonic and is applied to boils and carbuncles.

Zinc Gelatin Paste (Unna's paste) consists of zinc oxide and gelatin in glycerine and water. It is used for varicose lesions on the legs.

Zinc Oxide and Salicylic Acid Paste (Lassar's paste) contains zinc oxide and salicylic acid 2 per cent. It is used for chronic eczema and other scaly lesions.

Paints

Paints are preparations that dry rapidly when applied to the skin. Acetone, alcohol or ether, all of which dry rapidly, are commonly used as solvents for the active ingredient.

Coal Tar Paint contains crude coal tar 10 per cent in benzole and acetone. It is used for psoriasis and lichen simplex, and to relieve itching.

Compound Podophyllin Paint contains podophyllum resin. It is used for moist warts. It is very irritating to the eyes and care should be taken that none of it gets into them. It should be washed off the skin a few hours after application.

Crystal Violet Paint (Gentian violet paint) contains 0.5 per cent of crystal violet. It may be used as an antiseptic for weeping lesions.

Compound Crystal Violet Paint contains crystal violet and brilliant green. It may be used as an antiseptic for weeping lesions.

Antiseptics

Antiseptics are used to sterilize the skin before operation or injection or to sterilize surgical equipment and other utensils.

Cetrimide (Proprietary Name: Cetavlon) is an antiseptic and detergent and one of the 'quaternary ammonium compounds'. These compounds are effective against

Gram-positive organisms. As a solution or cream it is used to clean the skin before operation, to clean burns and wounds, to treat chronic skin diseases. Solutions of it are used to store sterile instruments and syringes and to clean utensils and linen. Instruments etc. stored in it must be carefully washed with sterile water or sterile normal saline before use. It is not effective against Gram-negative organisms, the tubercle bacillus and other organisms. To prevent infection of the fluid by these organisms, bottles of cetrimide must have screw-tops and not corks. Cetrimide's detergent properties are useful in the treatment of seborrheic dermatitis.

Benzalkonium Chloride Solution (Proprietary Name: Roccal) is another quaternary ammonium compound with antiseptic and detergent properties. Its actions and uses are similar to those of cetrimide. Lozenges of it are used for the treatment of throat infections.

Chlorhexidine (Proprietary Name: Hibitane) is effective against both Gram-positive and Gram-negative organisms. It is active in the presence of blood and other antiseptics. It can cause irritation of the conjunctiva and mucous membranes. Lozenges of it are used in the treatment of throat infections.

Tincture of Iodine (Weak Iodine Solution) is used to sterilize the skin before injections and operations. A 2 per cent solution of iodine in isopropyl alcohol is frequently used for this purpose.

Hypochlorite Solutions (such as Dakin's solution and Eusol) have been used for cleaning debris and pus from infected wounds and burns; they are applied by continuous or frequent irrigation. The surrounding skin must be protected by smearing it with soft paraffin.

Proflavine Hemisulphate (Proflavine) is an antiseptic effective against many Gram-positive and Gram-negative organisms. It is active in the presence of serum and pus, and may be used as a 1 in 1 000 solution for the treatment of 'dirty' wounds.

32 · Drugs for the Eye

Mydriatics are drugs that dilate the pupil of the eye. The ones used include:

(a) *Atropine* (atropine sulphate 1 per cent as drops or ointment). It produces a strong dilatation, but it acts slowly, starting to dilate the pupil in about 30 minutes; its effects may last for up to 7 days. In sensitive people an acute catarrhal conjunctivitis ('atropine irritation') can be produced. Atropine can precipitate an attack of glaucoma and for this reason must be used cautiously in old people.

(b) *Homatropine* (homatropine hydrobromide 2 per cent as drops). It acts more quickly than atropine and its effects are less powerful and prolonged; it is therefore more commonly used than atropine when the pupil is dilated for diagnostic purposes. It may be combined with cocaine hydrochloride 1 per cent to increase its action. Homatropine drops can cause delirium.

(c) *Hyoscine* (hyoscine hydrobromide 0.25 per cent as drops or ointment). Its action is less powerful than that of atropine.

(d) *Phenyl-ephrine* (phenyl-ephrine hydrochloride 10 per cent). It produces a wide dilatation of the pupil.

(e) *Lachesine* (lachesine chloride 1 per cent). It is used when a patient is sensitive to the atropine-homatropine group.

Miotics are drugs that cause constriction of the pupil of the eye. Among those used are:

(a) *Physostigmine Salicylate* (Eserine). It acts in about 5 minutes and is fully effective in 20–45 minutes. It is used to reduce the dilatation caused by homatropine and cocaine (it is not very effective against the dilatation caused by atropine); to treat glaucoma, solutions of 0.5–1.0 per cent are used. In some patients conjunctival smarting and 'dragging' is produced. Strong solutions can produce vomiting in some very sensitive patients.

(b) *Pilocarpine Nitrate* (0.25–5.0 per cent) is used in the treatment of glaucoma. It may be combined with physostigmine. Its action is not prolonged and may be followed by mydriasis (dilatation of the pupil).

Local Anaesthetics

Local anaesthesia of the eye may be produced by the application of an appropriate anaesthetic to the eye. Local anaesthetics used include:

(a) *Cocaine* (cocaine hydrochloride 2 per cent). C.D. It produces anaesthesia of the conjunctiva and cornea but not complete anaesthesia of the iris. It causes dilatation of the pupil. Some patients are very sensitive and can collapse after an application of cocaine to the conjunctiva.

(b) *Amethocaine* (amethocaine hydrochloride, tetracaine hydrochloride, 1 per cent). It does not dilate the pupil.

Antibiotics

Antibiotics can be administered as drops or ointments to treat infections of the eye by organisms susceptible to the drug. The ones used include:

(a) *Chloramphenicol* (0.5–1.0 per cent).

(b) *Tetracycline* (0.5 per cent), *Chlortetracycline* (1.0 per cent) and *Oxytetracycline* (1.0 per cent).

(c) *Neomycin* (0.5 per cent).

(d) *Framycetin* (0.5 per cent).

Eye Lotions

The following lotions are used as astringents or mild antiseptics or to remove conjunctival discharges.

(a) *Sodium Chloride* (1.8 per cent) as an eye-wash to remove conjunctival discharges.

(b) *Boric Acid* (3.4 per cent) as an eye-wash to remove conjunctival discharges.

(c) *Sodium Sulphacetamide* (Albucid). This sulphonamide is used as an ointment (6 per cent) or in drops (30 per cent). It does not cause irritation of the conjunctiva.

(d) *Sodium cromoglycate* (Opticrom Eye Drops) is given as drops to treat spring catarrh (vernal kerato-conjunctivitis).

Idoxuridine

Other name. I.D.U.

Proprietary name. Kerecid.

Actions and uses. It is an anti-metabolic drug which acts on certain viruses. It is used mainly for the treatment of infections of the cornea by herpes simplex, especially when a 'dendritic ulcer' is present. The recommended dose is 1 drop every hour by day and every 2 hours by night, reduced, when the ulcer is healed, to 1 drop every 2 hours by day and every 4 hours by night. These dosages should not be exceeded. The drug has also been used for local application to herpes simplex and herpes zoster infection of the skin.

Toxic and side effects. Some inflammation and irritation of the eyes may occur. A combination of idoxuridine with steroids is considered inadvisable as steroids increase the rate of spread of virus infections. The drug is contra-indicated in deep ulceration of the cornea for it may cause a perforation of the cornea.

Vidarabine Ophthalmic Ointment

Other Names. Adenine arabinoside, Ara-A.

Proprietary Name. Vira-A.

Dose. 1 cm of ointment applied to conjunctiva 5 times a day until new epithelium has covered cornea; then 3 times a day for 7 days.

Actions and Uses. It is an antiviral drug ointment effective against DNA viruses and used in the treatment of ulcerative herpetitic keratitis and herpetic corneal ulceration.

Toxic and Side Effects. Irritation, weeping, conjunctivitis, stenosis of lacrimal puncta.

33 · Drugs for the Ear, Nose and Throat

Drugs for the Ear

Acute infections of the middle ear are treated by the administration of antibiotics systemically, i.e. injected into the body or taken by mouth. Local chemotherapy may become necessary as well when perforation of the ear drum has occurred and in chronic otorrhoea. The precise antibiotic to be used is decided by testing the sensitivity of the organism to several antibiotics. Prolonged use of antibiotic drugs in ear-drops may lead to the growth of resistant strains of the infecting organism.

Other ear-drops are used to soften wax in the ear or to dry up any discharging surface in the meatus. Infections of the external ear are treated by the local application of antibiotic or other ear-drops or other local applications.

Antibiotic Ear-Drops

Chloramphenicol Ear Drops (Proprietary Preparations: Chloromycetin, Otophen) are given in a 10 per cent solution twice or three times a day. The drug is active against many organisms.

Hydrocortisone and Neomycin Ear Drops (Proprietary Preparation: Neo-Cortef) contain hydrocortisone acetate 1.5 per cent and neomycin sulphate 0.5 per cent. They are applied twice or three times a day.

Other Ear Preparations

Aluminium Acetate Ear Drops (Other Name: Burrow's solution) contain 13 per cent of aluminium acetate and are used as astringents, i.e. to dry up the meatus.

Boric Acid Ear Drops contain 2 per cent of boric acid in industrial methylated spirit and water and are used to clean the meatus when an infection has settled down.

Hydrogen Peroxide Ear Drops contain 25 per cent of hydrogen peroxide solution in water and are used to clear debris out of the meatus and to soften wax, the meatus being afterwards syringed with boric lotion.

Phenol Ear Drops contain 7.5 per cent of phenol in glycerin. They are used for their anaesthetic and antiseptic properties. These drops must not be mixed with water because the mixture then becomes caustic.

Sodium Bicarbonate Ear Drops contain 5 per cent of sodium bicarbonate in glycerin and water and are used to soften wax.

Spirit Ear Drops contain 50 per cent of industrial methylated spirit in water and are used to clean and dry the meatus when an infection has settled down.

Drugs for the Nose

Inhalations are used to clear the air passages, to reduce swollen mucous membranes in the nose, to treat spasm, and to relieve tracheitis, bronchitis and sinusitis. The patient inhales the vapour produced by adding one teaspoonful of the drug to a pint of hot water. The drugs used are menthol, benzoin, menthol and benzoin, and menthol and eucalyptus. The steam is probably more effective than any of the drugs.

Solutions for Nasal Application may be given as sprays, douches or drops applied to the nose twice or three times a day. They are used for the relief of nasal allergy, rhinitis, sinusitis, and eustachian tube obstruction, and to soften debris after operations on the nose and sinuses. *Ephedrine nasal drops* (which contain ½–2 per cent of ephedrine) are employed to relieve nasal congestion and promote drainage of the sinuses. Prolonged use of nasal applications may make the congestion worse. Oily nasal drops or sprays and liquid paraffin are not introduced into the nose because if they are inhaled into the lungs they can produce pneumonitis and pneumonia.

Sodium cromoglycate (Rynacrom) can be given as a nasal spray or as nasal drops to prevent allergic rhinitis. Some irritation of the nasal mucous membrane may occur at first. There are no contra-indications.

Eskornade

Dose. Adults: 1 capsule every 12 hours or 10 ml of syrup 3 times a day.

Children 1–6 years: 2.5 ml of syrup 3 times a day.

Children 7 years and older: 5 ml of syrup 3 times a day.

Actions and uses. This is a sustained release preparation containing isopropamide iodide, phenylpropanolamine and diphenylpyraline. It is a nasal decongestant and antihistaminic given orally.

Toxic and side effects. Drowsiness can occur; patients who drive or operate machinery should be warned of this. Other effects are blurred vision, retention of urine, constipation, palpitations, dizziness, insomnia.

Contra-indications: glaucoma, intestinal obstruction or atrophy, enlarged prostate gland, urinary retention, severe ulcerative colitis, hypertension, severe heart disease, hyperthyroidism, sensitivity to iodine. Treatment with a MAOI drug should not start within 14 days of taking Eskornade.

Drugs for the Throat

Gargles and lozenges are used for the relief of discomfort or pain in tonsillitis and pharyngitis. Several kinds of gargles are in use (including potassium chlorate, phenol, and ferric chloride). The drug may not penetrate the tissues, but the movements of gargling aid secretion from them. Lozenges are used to treat minor infections. Lozenges of benzocaine produce anaesthesia in the pharynx. Lozenges containing penicillin are harmful and should not be used.

Mandl's Paint (Compound iodine paint: it contains potassium iodide and iodine in glycerin, water and alcohol) is applied in the treatment of pharyngitis and Vincent's angina.

34 · Drugs for Gout and Rheumatism

Colchicine is a specific drug for the relief of attacks of gout; other drugs prevent attacks of gout by reducing the amount of uric acid in the blood. Sodium salicylate is used in the treatment of acute rheumatic fever. Several drugs (such as phenylbutazone) are used in the treatment of rheumatoid arthritis, osteo-arthritis and other diseases of joints.

Colchicine

Dose. Prevention: 500 mcg–1 mg daily.
  Treatment: Initial dose, 1 mg; subsequent doses, 500 mcg every 2 hours.

Actions and uses. It is an alkaloid obtained from the colchicum plant (autumn crocus). It is used in the prevention and treatment of gout. For acute gout it is given in the above doses until either relief from pain is obtained or diarrhoea or vomiting occur. It can be given by intravenous injection (in doses of 2–4 mg).

Toxic and side effects. Large doses can produce diarrhoea and vomiting.

Ketoprofen

Proprietary Names. Alrheumat, Orudis.

Dose. 50 mg 2–4 times daily with food.

Actions and uses. It is an anti-inflammatory drug used in the treatment of arthritis, ankylosing spondylitis, gout, bursitis, synovitis and other painful musculo-skeletal conditions.

Toxic and side effects. No serious side effects are known. In common with other anti-inflammatory drugs it is used cautiously with patients who have a history of peptic ulcer or impaired liver function.

Allopurinol

Proprietary name. Zyloric.

Dose. 200–600 mg daily in divided doses.

Actions and uses. It is an inhibitor of xanthine oxidase, an enzyme important in changing hypoxanthine into xanthine and xanthine into uric acid. Allopurinol prevents the change into uric acid, and hypoxanthine and xanthine are excreted by the kidney. The amount of uric acid in the blood is reduced and attacks of gout are prevented. The drug is used in the treatment of gout and to prevent the formation of urate stones in the renal tract. If another uricosuric drug is being given, it can be replaced gradually, over a month, by allopurinol; taking a patient off the other suddenly can precipitate an attack of gout. A daily output of 2 litres of urine is essential during treatment. The drug is also used to prevent deposits of stones in the renal tract during the treatment of neoplastic hyperuricaemia with anti-mitotic drugs or radiotherapy.

Toxic and side effects. Attacks of gout may be precipitated at the beginning of treatment, and colchicine should be given simultaneously. Fever, rashes, nausea, abdominal pain and diarrhoea can occur. Some patients develop enlargement of the liver and jaundice. A hypersensitivity syndrome can occur, consisting of a rash, fever, hepatitis and nephritis; it can cause death and should be promptly treated with steroids.

Probenecid

Proprietary name. Benemid.

Dose. 1–2 g daily.

Actions and uses. It increases the excretion of urates from the body by reducing tubular reabsorption in the kidneys. By decreasing the amount of uric acid in the blood, it reduces the number of attacks of gout and prevents the formation of gouty nodules (tophi). It has no effect on acute attacks of gout (which are treated by colchicine), and in the early weeks of treatment it may precipitate acute attacks. Treatment has to be continued for life. Alkalis (such as potassium citrate or sodium bicarbonate) should be taken regularly to prevent the formation of urate crystals in the kidneys.

As it reduces the excretion of penicillin by the kidneys, it can be used to maintain a high level of penicillin in the blood, as may be necessary in the treatment of subacute bacterial endocarditis.

Toxic and side effects. If nausea or vomiting occur, the dose of the drug should be reduced. If a skin rash or fever occurs, the drug should be discontinued.

Sulphinpyrazone

Proprietary name. Anturan.

Dose. 50–400 mg daily.

Actions and uses. It increases the excretion of urates from the body by reducing tubular reabsorption in the kidneys. By decreasing the amount of uric acid in the blood it reduces the number of attacks of gout and reduces the size of gouty nodules (tophi). It is more effective than probenecid. Like probenecid it has no action on acute attacks of gout. Treatment has to be continued indefinitely. The urine should be made alkaline by potassium acetate. Citrates and salicylates should not be given at the same time as they reduce its efficiency.

Toxic and side effects. It has to be given with care if renal function is impaired. It is contra-indicated in active peptic ulcer.

Sodium Salicylate

Dose. 5–10 g daily in divided doses.

Actions and uses. It is used in the treatment of acute rheumatic fever, doses being given every 2 or 3 hours until the temperature has fallen to normal. Sodium bicarbonate should not be given at the same time because it increases its excretion and so reduces its effectiveness.

Toxic and side effects. It is contra-indicated if there is heart-failure, and has to be given with care if there is acute renal disease. Some patients are very sensitive to it, even in small doses, and complain of ringing in the ears, dimness of vision, headache, mental confusion, rashes, sweating, and shortness of breath.

Phenylbutazone

Proprietary names. Butazolidin, Irgapyrin (with amido-pyrine), Tanderil (oxyphenbutazone).

Dose. 200–400 mg daily in divided doses.

Actions and uses. It relieves pain and fever. It is used in the treatment of rheumatism, rheumatoid arthritis, osteo-arthritis, spondylitis and gout.

Toxic and side effects. Toxic effects occur in many patients. They can occur with ordinary therapeutic doses and are particularly liable to occur if doses larger than those given above are administered. They include: (a) gastro intestinal disturbance, with ulceration of mucous membranes, haematemesis and melaena, (b) oedema of the tissues, (c) agranulocytosis and aplastic anaemia. The patient should be instructed to report to his doctor if he feels ill in any way. The drug is contra-indicated in peptic ulcer, cardiac failure, or any renal or hepatic disease. The gastro-intestinal disturbance is relieved by antacid treatment.

Indomethacin

Proprietary name. Indocid.

Dose. 25–100 mg daily in divided doses after meals.
    As suppository: 100 mg.

Actions and uses. It is a non-corticosteroid drug with
    anti-pyretic, pain-relieving and anti-inflammatory
    properties. It is used in the treatment of rheumatoid
    arthritis, osteo-arthritis, ankylosing spondylitis and
    gout. It may be given in combination with a cortico-
    steroid drug.

Toxic and side effects. Headache and giddiness occur
    commonly; abdominal discomfort and rashes occur less
    commonly. If doses larger than the above are given there
    is a risk of producing a peptic ulcer and bleeding from
    the stomach or intestine. It should not be given to a
    patient who has an active peptic ulcer or is pregnant.

Ibuprofen

Proprietary name. Brufen.

Dose. 200-400 mg three times a day.

Actions and uses. It is a non-steroid anti-rheumatic drug
    with pain-relieving and anti-inflammatory properties,
    used in the treatment of rheumatoid arthritis and
    osteo-arthritis.

Toxic and side effects. Gastric upsets, bronchospasm and
    a rash can occur.

Hydroxychloroquine Sulphate

Proprietary name. Plaquenil.

Dose. For rheumatoid arthritis: Initial dose: 400–600 mg.
Maintenance dose: 200–400 mg.

Actions and uses. It is an anti-malarial drug which also
acts on rheumatoid arthritis, lupus erythematosus and
some other conditions. How it acts in collagen diseases
is not definitely known. Treatment has to be continued
over several months. It does not relieve pain and can be
combined with an analgesic (such as aspirin) or, if
necessary, with a cortico-steroid.

Toxic and side effects. Prolonged administration, which is
necessary, may produce: (a) corneal opacities: treatment should be stopped or temporarily suspended until
they clear up; (b) pigment disturbances in the retina
and a reduction in the visual fields: treatment must be
stopped; (c) bone marrow changes leading to agranulocytosis and aplastic anaemia: regular blood counts are
done and treatment is stopped if blood-formation
becomes depressed; (d) skin rashes of various kinds,
alopecia and bleaching of hair: treatment is stopped
until they clear up; (e) gastro intestinal disturbances,
which should clear up when drug is suspended; (f)
muscle weakness and loss of tendon reflexes; treatment
is stopped. The drug is used cautiously with patients
who have psoriasis, gastro-intestinal, blood or neurological disease.

Sodium Auriothiomalate

Proprietary name. Myocrisin.

Dose. Initial dose of 5–10 mg given intramuscularly and increased up to 50 mg weekly.

Actions and uses. It is a gold salt used in the treatment of rheumatoid arthritis and chronic discoid lupus erythematosus. Treatment may have to be continued for 3 months before there is any apparent improvement. A monthly maintenance dose may be given. A monthly blood-count should be done and the urine tested for albumin.

Toxic and side effects. Dermatitis, thrombocytopenia and aplasia of bone-marrow may occur and have to be treated immediately by dimercaprol (BAL) and corticosteroids. Contra-indications: severe kidney or liver disease, bleeding diseases, severe diabetes.

Alclofenac

Dose. 500 mg three times a day, reducing to 500 mg daily.

Actions and uses. It has pain-relieving and anti-inflammatory properties, and is used in the treatment of arthritis, rheumatism and chronic pain.

Toxic and side effects. A rash, nausea and indigestion can occur.

35 · Radio-Isotopes

An isotope is an element of the same atomic number as another but of a different atomic weight.

Radio-isotopes are isotopes that have been made radio-active by bombarding an element with neutrons, protons, etc. at an Atomic Centre. The radioactive isotope emits radiations (in the form of alpha-particles, beta-particles or gamma-rays) from the nucleus of the atom. These radiations in time die out, and the rate at which they die out is expressed as its 'half life', i.e. the period of time in which its radioactivity becomes half its original strength.

Radio-isotopes can be used to diagnose or to treat certain diseases.

A micro-curie is one-millionth of a curie. A milli-curie is one-thousandth of a curie.

Chromium-51

Other name. ^{51}Cr.

Half-life. 27 days.

Dose. 50–100 μc.

Actions and uses. It is given as *Sodium Chromate* (^{51}Cr.) *Injection*, a sterile solution of its sodium salt. It is used (in a dose of about 50 μc) to determine red blood cell volume, and (in a dose of about 100 μc) to diagnose haemolytic anaemia.

Iodine-131

Other name. ^{131}I.

Half-life. 8 days.

Dose. To assess thyroid function: 5–50 μc.
  To treat hyperthyroidism: 5–15 μc.
  To treat carcinoma of the thyroid gland: 60–100 mc.

Actions and uses. It is given by mouth as a solution of the sodium salt. The greater the activity of the thyroid gland, the greater is the amount of radioactive iodine taken up by it. The amount taken up is measured by a Geiger-counter placed on the skin of the neck over the thyroid gland. Some of the iodine-131 is excreted in the urine; and the amount excreted in the urine is sometimes measured, because the more radioactive iodine is taken up by the thyroid gland, the less is excreted by the kidneys. Potassium iodide or other iodine-containing drugs must not have been given before, because they can interfere with the urine test.

  Radioactive iodine interferes with the functioning of the thyroid cells, and can be used in the treatment of hyperthyroidism and carcinoma of the thyroid gland.

Toxic and side effects. Over-dosage can, by destroying thyroid tissue, produce myxoedema or by irritating the tissues can produce carcinoma of the thyroid gland. It is contra-indicated in childhood, during pregnancy, and when a woman is breast-feeding a child.

Iodine-132

Other name. ^{132}I.

Half-life. 2½ hours.

Actions and uses. This radio-isotope is used in diagnostic tests of thyroid function. Its life being very short (its radio-activity has almost completely disappeared within 24 hours), it has to be prepared in combination with another isotope (tellurium-132) in such a way that it can be ready for use when required.

Phosphorus-32

Other name. ^{32}P.

Half-life. 14 days.

Dose. 3–5 mc by intravenous injection.

Actions and uses. It is given as *Sodium Phosphate (^{32}P) Injection*, a sterile solution of its sodium salt. It gives off beta-rays and is used in the treatment of poly-cythaemia vera and chronic myeloid leukaemia and diagnostically to localize tumours in the brain and else-where, and to estimate the length of the life of red blood cells.

Toxic and side effects. As it depresses the bone-marrow, it can produce aplastic anaemia, a reduction of the number of white cells, and purpura. It is contra-indi-cated in severe anaemia, leucopenia, when there is a reduction in the number of blood-platelets and in pregnancy.

36 · Drugs for Malignant Disease

Several drugs are now available for the treatment of malignant disease. They are sometimes referred to as anti-mitotic drugs (mitosis – division of cells into other cells) or cytotoxic drugs (i.e. drugs that harm cells). They act by interfering in one way or another with cell division. Cancer cells, which are multiplying rapidly, are therefore particularly liable to be affected by them, but to some extent also are other cells which are in fairly rapid production, such as the cells of the blood and cells of the mucous membrane of the gastro-intestinal tract. Side effects are therefore to be expected in the blood and gastro intestinal system. Some anti-mitotic drugs are derivatives of mustard gas; some synthetic drugs with anti-mitotic properties have been produced. In general, all these drugs produce only temporary improvement and do not effect a cure. But they prolong life and greatly relieve symptoms. They may be combined with surgery when surgery is possible or given without it when surgery is impossible or inadvisable; they may be combined with radiotherapy. They should not be given in pregnancy as they can cause severe fetal abnormalities.

One method of giving these drugs is by 'regional perfusion', blood containing the drug being circulated through the part of the body affected with a malignant growth by means of a pump-oxygenator for an hour or more. This is most easily done for the limbs, which can be isolated from the rest of the body, but it has been applied to other parts such as the head, breast and the pelvis.

Other drugs used in the treatment of malignant disease are: (a) oestrogens and androgens in hormone-dependent tumours, e.g. stilboestrol for carcinoma of the prostate gland, and (b) prednisolone in acute leukaemia.

Busulphan

Proprietary name. Myleran.

Dose. Initial dose: 2–6 mg daily.
   Maintenance dose: 500 mcg–2 mg daily.

Actions and uses. It interferes with cell-division, especially in the bone-marrow. It is chiefly used in the treatment of myeloid leukaemia. The number of white cells becomes reduced, the enlarged spleen shrinks, and anaemia is relieved. A dose of 2–6 mg daily may have to be given for 3 months to produce the maximum improvement, and then the smaller maintenance dose can be given. A complete blood-count should be done weekly.

Toxic and side effects. Like other drugs in this group, it affects the growth of normal tissues. In particular, the number of platelets is likely to be reduced, and when this happens thrombocytopenia is produced. A condition resembling Addison's disease (pigmentation of skin, loss of weight, fatigue, loss of appetite, nausea) has been produced. Cataract and fibrosis of the lungs are other complications of long-term treatment.

Mithramycin

Dose. 15 mcg per kilo of body-weight given in 500 ml 5 per cent dextrose by intravenous infusion over 4–5 days with intervals of 5 days between courses.

Actions and uses. It is an antibiotic used in the treatment of (a) tumours, because it has cell-destroying properties, and (b) osteitis deformans (Paget's disease) because it stimulates the release of para-thyroid hormone.

Chlorambucil

Proprietary name. Leukeran.

Dose. 0.2 mg per kilo body weight daily.

Actions and uses. It interferes with chromosome development in the nuclei of cells, especially lymphocytes, neutrophil granulocytes and platelets. It is used in the treatment of Hodgkin's disease, lymphosarcoma and lymphatic leukaemia. It should not be given within 4 weeks of treatment by x-rays or any other cytotoxic drug. Short courses of treatment with a larger dose of the drug may be given, or alternatively a continuous course of a smaller, maintenance dose. A full blood-count is done weekly; the mucous membranes and skin are examined weekly for any haemorrhages into them.

Toxic and side effects. Over-dosage produces a reduction of white cells and platelets below the normal levels.

Cyclophosphamide

Proprietary names. Endoxana, Endoxan.

Dose. By intravenous injection: 100 mg as first dose; increased daily by 200–400 mg until a total of 5–7 g has been given.
    By mouth: 50–100 mg daily.

Actions and uses. It is a substance from which nitrogen mustard is released after its absorption. It is used in the treatment of Hodgkin's disease, leukaemia and malignant reticuloses. Weekly blood-counts are done. Maintenance doses can be administered by mouth.

Toxic and side effects. Nausea and vomiting may follow the injection. The hair may fall out, but usually grows again. Leucopenia can be produced. Acute cystitis, haematuria and with high doses fibrosis of the bladder can occur.

Mercaptopurine

Proprietary name. Puri-Nethol.

Dose. 2.5 mg per kilo of body-weight daily by mouth.
Can be increased to 5 mg per kilo of body-weight daily by mouth after 4 weeks' continuous treatment.

Actions and uses. It is used in combination with other drugs in the treatment of acute leukaemia. It is sometimes of value in the treatment of chronic myeloid leukaemia. A complete blood-count should be done weekly.

Toxic and side effects. If the number of leucocytes falls below normal or anaemia is produced, the dose of the drug should be reduced or it should be stopped altogether. Gastro-intestinal disturbance and ulceration of the mouth can occur.

Thiotepa

Dose. 2–4 mg per kilo of body-weight intramuscularly.

Actions and uses. It is used in the palliative treatment of malignant disease. The above dose is given over a period of 2–4 weeks. It can also be given intravenously, intra-arterially, by perfusion or infusion, directly into a tumour or into a pleural cavity when there is a malignant effusion.

Toxic and side effects. It can produce mental depression and a depression of bone activities.

Methotrexate

Proprietary name. Methotrexate.

Dose. By mouth: 2.5–5 mg daily at first; followed by maintenance doses of 5–10 mg weekly.

By intra-thecal injection 250–500 mcg per kilo body-weight.

Actions and uses. It is a cytotoxic drug used especially in the treatment of acute leukaemia; intrathecal injections are used to treat leukaemic meningeal deposits in childhood. It is also used to treat cancer of the testis and chorion-carcinoma.

It is also used to treat severe psoriasis in men who do not wish to have children and in women after the menopause.

Toxic and side effects. It can produce loss of hair, ulcers in the mouth and jaundice and interfere with blood-cell production by bone-marrow. Prolonged administration in the treatment of psoriasis can cause cirrhosis of the liver.

Vinblastine Sulphate

Proprietary name. Velbe.

Dose. 100–200 mcg per kilo body-weight by weekly intravenous injection.

Actions and uses. It is one of a number of drugs derived from plants which by damaging the chromosomes in cell-nuclei prevent the multiplication of cells. It is used in the treatment of leukaemia, Hodgkin's disease and chorion-carcinoma.

Vincristine is a similar preparation given in combination with other drugs.

Toxic and side effects. Both drugs can damage the bone-marrow and cause peripheral neuropathy.

Procarbazine

Proprietary name. Natulan.

Dose. Initial treatment: 50 mg on 1st day; increased by 50 mg daily up to maximum of 250–300 mg daily.
Maintenance dose: 50–150 mg daily.

Actions and uses. It is used in the treatment of Hodgkin's disease, other advanced reticuloses, and several kinds of tumour.

Toxic and side effects. Loss of appetite, nausea and vomiting are common at the beginning of treatment and are not indications for stopping it. Bone-marrow function is depressed: treatment is suspended if the white cell count falls below 3 000 per c.mm. or the platelet count below 80 000 per c.mm.; it is resumed with maintenance doses when the count is normal. It may potentiate barbiturates, phenothiazine derivatives and drugs of the imipramine type. The patient should be warned not to take alcohol. Treatment is stopped if allergic skin reactions occur.

Doxorubicin

Proprietary name. Adriamycin.

Dose. 400–800 mcg per kg body-weight in intravenous infusion.

Actions and uses. It is an antimitotic and cytotoxic antibiotic used for various kinds of neoplasm.

Toxic and side effects. As for other similar drugs.

Daunorubicin

Proprietary name. Cerubidin.

Dose. A single dose of 3 mg per kilo body-weight given intravenously.

Actions and uses. It is an antibiotic given in the treatment of acute leukaemia. How it acts is not known.

CIS-Platin

Other name. DDP.

Proprietary name. Neoplatin.

Dose. Various schemes of intravenous treatment, e.g. daily bolus injection for 5 days, 5-day continuous infusion, 24-hour infusion.

Actions and uses. This is a platinum compound which stops the growth of cells. It is effective against germ-cell tumours of the testis, and has been used to treat cancer of the ovary, bladder, etc.

Toxic and side effects. Nausea, vomiting; renal damage; hearing loss, tinnitus; anaemia; anaphylactic-like reactions; peripheral neuropathy; excessive loss of magnesium in urine.

37 · Heavy Metal Antagonists

Heavy metal antagonists are drugs which promote the excretion from the body of metals such as antimony, arsenic, copper and lead.

Dimercaprol

Other names. British Anti-Lewisite, BAL.

Dose. First day: 400 mg by intramuscular injection.
  Second, third and fourth days: 200 mg.
  Fifth and sixth days: 100 mg daily.

Actions and uses. It is a heavy metal antagonist, which reacts with certain heavy metals, converts them into inactive forms, and enables them to be excreted. It is used in the treatment of acute poisoning by antimony, arsenic, bismuth, gold, mercury and thallium. It is not effective in the treatment of poisoning by cadmium, iron and lead.

Toxic and side effects. It can cause nausea, vomiting, weeping, salivation, burning sensations in the mouth, throat and eyes, headache, feelings of constriction in the throat and chest, and a rise of blood-pressure. Injections are painful.

Penicillamine Hydrochloride

Dose. 1–1.5 g daily in divided doses.

Actions and uses. It is a heavy-metal antagonist. Its chief use is the treatment of hepato-lenticular degeneration (Wilson's disease) by promoting the excretion of copper in the urine. It can also be used in the treatment of poisoning by lead and mercury.

Toxic and side effects. Nausea, vomiting and allergic reactions can occur, but are not usually an indication for stopping treatment. A myasthenia gravis-like syndrome can develop with long-term treatment.

Sodium Calciumedetate

Proprietary names. Calcium Disodium Versenate, EDTA.

Dose. Up to 3 g daily by mouth.
   By intravenous injection: see below.

Actions and uses. It is a heavy-metal antagonist used in
   the treatment of lead poisoning. It forms a compound
   of lead which is excreted in the urine.

   It can be given by intravenous injection as a 0.2–3 per
   cent solution with dextrose or sodium chloride, for one
   hour twice daily for up to 5 days. The treatment can be
   repeated after 2–3 days have elapsed. It can be given by
   mouth.

Toxic and side effects. Prolonged administration can
   damage the kidneys. The blood-calcium level can be
   lowered.

Desferrioxamine B Mesylate

Proprietary name. Desferal.

Dose. 5 g in 50–100 ml fluid, followed by 2 g intramuscularly, and then by slow intravenous injection.

Actions and uses. It combines with iron to form non-toxic
   compounds, which are excreted in the urine. It is used
   in the treatment of acute iron poisoning. It is also used
   to detect excessive storage of iron in the body as in
   haemochromatosis.

Toxic and side effects. Intravenous injection can cause
   anaphylactic reactions. Pyelonephritis can be made
   worse by the excretion of iron by the kidneys.

38 · Gases and Anaesthetics

Oxygen

Actions and uses. It is given to relieve anoxia (shortage of oxygen), e.g. congestive heart failure, pneumonia, poisoning by carbon monoxide, morphine or barbiturates. It may be administered by means of a face-mask, a nasal catheter or an oxygen tent. It is frequently given in combination with carbon dioxide 5–7 per cent when stimulation of the respiratory centre in the brain is required.

It is stored in cylinders painted white on the shoulder and black on the rest of the cylinder; 'O$_2$' is stencilled on the shoulders. Oxygen and carbon dioxide mixtures have cylinders with the shoulders marked with 2 grey and 2 white segments.

Toxic and side effects. Given in excessive amounts and for too long to premature babies, oxygen can produce blindness by causing the blood vessels to increase in number, so causing the condition called retrolental fibroplasia.

Carbon Dioxide

Actions and uses. Carbon dioxide is a stimulant of the respiratory centre in the brain. It is given as a 5–7 per cent mixture with oxygen to stimulate respiration, e.g. in poisoning by carbon monoxide, barbiturates or morphine. The mixture can be used to stop chronic hiccup.

It is stored in cylinders painted grey all over with 'CO$_2$' stencilled on the shoulders. Mixtures of it with oxygen have cylinders with 2 grey and 2 white segments on the shoulders, the rest of the cylinder being painted black.

Solid carbon dioxide (in the form of a 'stick') is used to destroy warts and naevi. The pointed end of a 'stick' is pressed on the wart or naevus for 5–6 seconds.

Cyclopropane

Other name. Trimethylene.

Actions and uses. It is an anaesthetic gas, which acts quickly and is not irritant. It is normally administered in a closed circuit in combination with oxygen. A cyclopropane-oxygen mixture is highly explosive. It must not be given in the presence of naked flame or of any electrical apparatus that gives off a spark; precautions must be taken that static electricity is not produced.

It is stored in cylinders painted orange all over and with 'Cyclopropane' or C_3H_6' stencilled on the shoulder.

Toxic and side effects. It is a respiratory depressant. It can cause spasm of the bronchi, irregular beating of the heart, and an increase in any haemorrhage that may be occurring. Adrenaline should not be given to a patient while he is anaesthetized by it. Post-operatively a fall of blood-pressure or lung collapse can occur. Repeated anaesthesia by it can damage the liver and so make the patient jaundiced.

Ether

Other name. Anaesthetic ether.

Actions and uses. It is a volatile anaesthetic. As anaesthesia by it is produced slowly, it is a common practice to induce anaesthesia with another anaesthetic, e.g. thiopentone. It is highly inflammable. It must not be given in the presence of a naked flame or any electrical apparatus that gives off a spark; precautions must ensure that static electricity is not produced.

Toxic and side effects. It can produce laryngeal spasm. It produces salivation and excessive secretion from the bronchi, and atropine is given before operation to prevent these effects.

Vinyl Ether

Other name. Divinyl Ether

Proprietary name. Vinesthene.

Actions and uses. It is a volatile anaesthetic, usually used to induce anaesthesia or as a short-term anaesthetic for minor operations or to reinforce anaesthesia by nitrous oxide and oxygen. It acts rapidly. It does not usually produce muscular relaxation.

Toxic and side effects. Salivation can be troublesome. Cyanosis is produced by over-dosage. Repeated administration of it can damage the liver. The drug should be discarded if the ampoule containing it has been open for more than 48 hours.

Halothane

Proprietary name. Fluothane.

Actions and uses. It is a volatile anaesthetic usually administered in a special apparatus designed to administer it at a certain vapour-pressure.

It produces anaesthesia rapidly. It relaxes muscles to some extent; other muscle-relaxants (see p. 223) have to be used cautiously with it. Recovery from anaesthesia is rapid; vomiting does not usually occur. It is not inflammable and mixtures of it with oxygen are not explosive.

Toxic and side effects. Irregularities of the heart action can occur during induction. Overdosage produces respiratory depression, a fall in blood-pressure, and slowness of the pulse.

Nitrous Oxide

Actions and uses. It is a rapidly acting anaesthetic. Given by itself, it produces anoxia (with cyanosis, slow respiration, and dilated pupils) and is only suitable for very short operations, e.g. a dental extraction. For longer operations it is given in combination with oxygen 10 per cent.

Toxic and side effects. Toxic effects are produced when it is given without oxygen and are due to anoxia (lack of oxygen).

Nitrous Oxide and Oxygen

Proprietary name. Entonox.

Actions and uses. A 50/50 gaseous mixture of nitrous oxide and oxygen in one cylinder is used for the relief of pain in childbirth and dental anaesthesia. If the cylinder is exposed to a temperature of —8°C or lower, the amount of oxygen drawn off is increased and this causes the concentration of nitrous oxide to increase. Cylinders exposed to this dergee of cold should be turned upside down smartly 3 or 4 times; this action restores the proportion of gases to the correct one.

The body of the cylinder is blue, the neck is half-white, half-blue, and the top is stencilled '50% N_2O 50%O_2'.

Thiopentone Sodium

Other names. Soluble thiopentone, thiopental sodium.

Proprietary names. Intraval Sodium, Pentothal.

Actions and uses. It is an intravenous anaesthetic; 100–150 mg in a 5 per cent solution produces anaesthesia in about 30 seconds. The patient must be lying down. It is used for short operations or to induce general anaesthesia, or repeated injections or continuous administration are given. It can be given in combination with a muscle relaxant (see p. 223); it must not be mixed in the same syringe as suxamethonium, which it destroys. It can be given by rectum, in a dose of 40 mg per kilo of body-weight. Suppositories for inducing anaesthesia in children are available.

Toxic and side effects. It can cause respiratory depression. If it is injected by mistake into an artery, an immediate injection of 10 ml of procaine 1 per cent solution is made into the artery to prevent arterial spasm and gangrene. Injected outside a vein, it can cause degeneration of the tissues.

It is contra-indicated in patients with low blood-pressure, respiratory insufficiency, and liver disease.

Methohexitone Sodium

Proprietary name. Brietal.

Actions and uses. It is a barbiturate given intravenously as an anaesthetic for short operations for cardioversion (the restoration of normal heart rhythm by electric shock), and to induce anaesthesia for longer operations. It has been used with muscle relaxants in the treatment of status epilepticus.

Trichlorethylene

Proprietary name. Trilene.

Actions and uses. It is a volatile anaesthetic. It produces anaesthesia rapidly, but the anaesthesia is not very deep and muscular relaxation is not produced. It is therefore used for short operations not requiring muscular relaxation or to induce anaesthesia. It may be given in combination with air or oxygen with nitrous oxide. It has to be given in a suitable inhaler; it must not be given in a closed-circuit apparatus.

Toxic and side effects. It can produce rapid respiration and cardiac irregularities. Adrenaline must not be given to a patient anaesthetized with it.

Ketamine

Actions and uses. It is a non-barbiturate anaesthetic, acting in one minute when given intravenously and almost as quickly when given intramuscularly. The patient's eyes may remain open; muscle tone is increased and random movements may occur. It is useful for short operations and to induce anaesthesia. Vivid frightening dreams may occur during recovery.

39 · Neuro-Muscular Blocking Drugs

Neuro-muscular blocking drugs cause paralysis of voluntary muscles by blocking chemically the transmission of nervous impulses to muscles. Such paralysis is desirable during certain operations, during certain diagnostic procedures (e.g. bronchoscopy, laryngoscopy), in the reduction of fractures, in the treatment of tetanus and status epilepticus, and in electro-cerebral treatment (ECT) for mental disease. As the diaphragm and other muscles of respiration are paralysed along with the other skeletal muscles, an experienced staff and the necessary apparatus must be present in order that the air-way is kept clear and controlled respiration with adequate oxygenation is given for so long as the patient remains paralysed.

Fazadinium Bromide

Proprietary name. Fazadon.

Dose. 0.5 mg per kilo body weight for relaxation during anaesthesia.

0.75–1.0 mg per kilo body weight for intubation.

Actions and uses. It is a neuromuscular blocking agent used in tracheal intubation at the start of surgery and for muscular relaxation during abdominal surgery. It has a rapid action.

Toxic and side effects. Increase in heart rate; urticaria, wheezing; prolonged paralysis (up to 2 hours) after a large dose.

Suxamethonium Chloride

Proprietary names. Anectine, Brevidil M, Scoline, Quelicin, Sucastrin.

Dose. The usual single dose for an adult is 30–100 mg, intravenously, according to the physical development of the patient, the amount of anaesthetic required, and the expected length of the operation. For a long operation, repeated injections may be given.

Actions and uses. It is a relaxant of voluntary muscle, acting on the neuro-muscular junction. Administration of it is preceded by an intravenous anaesthetic. Short muscular contractions are followed by a paralysis which lasts for about 6 minutes. It is useful for short operative procedures and for ECT. The usual anaesthetics may be given (e.g. nitrous oxide, thiopentone, cyclopropane, ether). It must not be mixed in the same syringe as thiopentone, which destroys it. A clear air-way and adequate controlled respiration must be maintained.

Neostigmine is *not* an antidote.

Tubocurarine Chloride

Proprietary name. Tubarine.

Dose. 10–20 mg intravenously; subsequent doses of 2–4 mg at 30-minute intervals up to a total of 45 mg.

Actions and uses. It paralyses voluntary muscles by preventing the transmission of nervous impulses at the neuro-muscular junctions. It can be used with the usual anaesthetics. Paralysis begins to pass off after about 20 minutes.

Toxic and side effects. Respiratory failure can be prolonged. It is contra-indicated in myasthenia gravis. Neostigmine methylsulphate (2.5–5 mg) injected intravenously with atropine sulphate (500 mcg–1 mg) is an antidote.

Alcuronium Chloride

Proprietary name. Alloferin.

Dose. Adults: 10–15 mg intravenously.
    Children: 125–200 mcg per kilo body-weight.

Actions and uses. It is a curare-derivative, producing muscle relaxation, which begins in 3–4 minutes and lasts for 15–20. A second dose of 3–5 mg can be given.

Toxic and side effects. It should not be given in the same syringe as thiopentone. Prostigmin 500 mcg–1.0 mg is an antidote.

Gallamine Triethiodide

Other name. Gallamine.

Proprietary names. Flaxedil, Flaxedil Triethiode.

Dose. Usual initial dose 60–80 mg intravenously; further doses may be necessary up to a total of 120 mg.

Actions and uses. It paralyses voluntary muscles by preventing the transmission of nervous impulses at the neuro-muscular junctions. It is injected intravenously, acts within about 1 minute, and continues to be effective for about 20 minutes. It can be given with the usual anaesthetics (e.g. nitrous oxide, thiopentone, cyclopropane, ether).

Toxic and side effects. It can cause prolonged tachycardia. It is contra-indicated in myasthenia gravis. Neostigmine methylsulphate (2.5–5 mg) injected intravenously with atropine sulphate (500 mcg–1 mg) is an antidote.

40 · Local Anaesthetics

Local anaesthetics are drugs that produce local anaesthesia when injected into the skin, applied to a mucous membrane, or injected by lumbar puncture.

Cocaine

Dose. For the eyes: 2 per cent solution.
   For the larynx: 10–20 per cent solution.
   For the ear and nose: 5–10 per cent solution.

Actions and uses. As it has serious toxic effects and readily becomes a drug of addiction, cocaine is used as a local anaesthetic only for operations on the eye or on the ear, nose and throat. Anaesthesia develops in 5–10 minutes and persists for 30 minutes or longer.

Toxic and side effects. Some people are very sensitive to cocaine, even in the small amounts used in local anaesthesia. Excitement, over-activity and pyrexia may occur. The patient may faint, collapse or even die.

Procaine Hydrochloride

Other names. Ethocaine, allocaine, syncaine.

Proprietary names. Novutox, Planocaine.

Dose. For injection of the skin: 0.2–2 per cent solution.
   For nerve-block: 2 per cent solution.

Actions and uses. It is a short-acting local anaesthetic, often combined with a dilute solution of adrenaline (1 in 50 000), which by constricting local blood-vessels allows the anaesthetic action to be localized and prolonged. Procaine is given by injection. It is not applied to mucous membranes because so little is absorbed.

Toxic and side effects. It is quickly destroyed in the body and does not usually produce any toxic or side effects.

Lignocaine Hydrochloride

Other name. Lidocaine hydrochloride.

Proprietary names. Fastocain, Xylocaine, Xylodase, Xylotox.

Dose. For injection: 0.25–2 per cent solution.
  For local application: 0.25–2 per cent solution.
  For epidural injection: 1–2 per cent solution.

Actions and uses. It acts rapidly and has a low toxicity. In some preparations it is combined with adrenaline to localize anaesthesia and increase its effect. The combination with adrenaline must never be given intravenously nor injected into the fingers or toes (because of the danger of causing gangrene).

Toxic and side effects. If the precautions described above are taken, toxic effects are not to be expected.

Cinchocaine Hydrochloride

Other name. Dibucaine.

Proprietary names. Dermacaine, Nupercainal, Nupercaine.

Dose. By injection: 0.03–0.1 per cent solution.
  Nerve-block: 0.1 per cent solution.
  Spinal block: 0.1–0.5 per cent solution.
  Local application: 0.5–2 per cent solution.

Actions and uses. It is a powerful local anaesthetic, used by injection, by local application to mucous membranes, or for spinal anaesthesia. It is effective in relatively low concentrations. It may be combined with adrenaline, but this combination must not be injected into fingers or toes (because of the danger of producing gangrene). It can be given as a lozenge to produce anaesthesia of the pharynx and larynx before diagnostic procedures. Suppositories of it can be used to treat the pain of haemorrhoids or of an anal fissure.

Toxic and side effects. It is a relatively safe local anaesthetic in the solutions given above, and with the precaution taken of not injecting into a finger or toe any combination of it with adrenaline.

41 · Sclerosing Agents

Sclerosing agents are drugs that are injected into the walls of veins or into the blood in the vein to produce reactions in the wall or clotting of the blood with the result that the vein becomes fibrosed.

Monoethylolamine Oleate

Proprietary name. Ethamolin.

Dose. 2–5 ml by intravenous injection.

Actions and uses. It is a sclerosing agent used in the treatment of varicose veins.

Toxic and side effects. Allergic reactions can occur, and because of this a solution of 1 : 1 000 adrenaline should be at hand, and a test dose of 0.5 ml of the drug should be given first. If the solution leaks into the tissues around the vein, an ulcer can be produced. The clot formed by the drug is very firm, and the risk of a fragment breaking off and forming an embolus is very slight.

Oily Phenol Injection

Other name. 5 per cent phenol in oil injection.

Dose. 0.5–1.5 ml by injection.

Actions and uses. The drug consists of a 5 per cent solution of phenol (carbolic acid) in almond oil; some menthol may be added to the solution. It is used in the treatment of haemorrhoids, being injected into their submucous layer. If there are several haemorrhoids, two or three treatments at fortnightly intervals are necessary.

Toxic and side effects. Sloughing of the tissues may occur if an injection is made into a submucous layer that has already become sclerosed.

42 · Anthelmintics

Anthelmintics are drugs used to treat infection by worms (helminths). The worms may be: (a) intestinal parasites – threadworms, roundworms, tapeworms or hookworms; (b) filaria, which live in the lymphatics, connective tissue and skin; and (c) schistosomes, which live in blood-vessels. Some drugs are specific for one type of worm, others act on several.

Piperazine

Other names. Piperazine adipate, piperazine citrate, piperazine phosphate.

Proprietary Names. Antepar, Pripsen.

Dose. Adults. For threadworms: 1–2 g daily in divided doses. For roundworms: a dose of 75 mg per kilo body-weight is given up to a maximum of 4 g.

Children. For threadworms: 1/4–1/3 the above doses according to age up to the age of 6 years; above 6 years, from one half the above dose to adult dose according to age. For roundworms: twice the above children's doses for threadworms given daily for four days (not in a single dose).

Actions and uses. In the treatment of the threadworm infection, a piperazine salt is given as either a tablet or an elixir (a flavoured solution). The worms are paralysed and expelled. Treatment has to be given for one week, then stopped for one week, and then given for another week. Strict cleanliness must be practised, the perianal region and buttocks being carefully washed after each bowel movement. All members of a family living in the same house should be treated at the same time.

In the treatment of roundworm infection, a single large dose is given to an adult and can be repeated the next day. Smaller doses are given over four days for children. The worm is paralysed and expelled from the bowel. If it is not expelled a purgative is given.

Toxic and side effects. In the recommended doses no toxic effects are to be expected. Excessive doses can produce vomiting, dizziness, blurred vision and ataxia ('worm wobble') of a cerebellar type with inco-ordination and hypotonia.

Viprynium

Proprietary name. Povan.

Dose. Up to 12 years: 5 mg per kilo of body-weight given as a single dose.

Actions and uses. Viprynium is effective against thread-worms only. It paralyses and expels them. It has the great advantage that only one dose need be given. The faeces are stained red. Nausea, vomiting and diarrhoea can occur.

Niclosamide

Proprietary name. Yomesan.

Dose. 1 g, followed by 1 g, 1 hour later.

Actions and uses. Niclosamide is used in the treatment of infection by the beef tapeworm (*Taenia saginata*). A purgative is not necessary.

Toxic and Side Effects. Some intestinal colic may occur.

Mepacrine Hydrochloride

Proprietary Names. Atebrin, Quinacrine.

Dose. 1 g.

Actions and Uses. It is used to treat tapeworm infections when other drugs have failed. The patient is admitted to hospital and given fluids only for 36–48 hours. Mepacrine 1 g in 40 ml water is injected down a duodenal tube. A saline purge is given 30 minutes later. The faeces of the next 24 hours are examined for the head of the worm.

Toxic and side effects. Some nausea and vomiting are to be expected.

Bephinium Hydroxynaphthoate

Proprietary names. Alcopar, Alcopara.

Dose. 5 g.

Actions and uses. The drug acts on hookworms
(*Ancylostoma* and *Necator*). The patients should be
fasted before treatment. The drug is given in suspension
in water. For *Ancylostoma* infections one dose is given.
For *Necator* infections several doses may have to be
given. The same drug acts on roundworms and whip-
worms.

Toxic and side effects. It is bitter and may cause vomiting
and loose stools.

Tetrachlorethylene

Dose. Adults: 3–5 ml in a single dose in a draught or
capsule.

Actions and uses. It is used in the treatment of hookworms.
The patient is fasted and purged with magnesium
sulphate; a single dose of the drug is then given. The
patient is not purged afterwards. A second dose of the
drug can be given if necessary 3 days later.

Toxic and side effects. Headache, abdominal pain and
giddiness can occur.

Diethylcarbamazine Citrate

Proprietary Names. Banocide, Ethodryl, Hetrazan.

Dose. 150–500 mg three times a day.

Actions and uses. This drug is related to piperazine (which is used in the treatment of threadworms). It is used in the treatment of the forms of filariasis caused by the micro-filariae of *W. bancrofti*, *Onchocerca*, *Brugia* and *Loa Loa*. It kills the adult worms and removes the micro-filariae from the blood. Treatment has to be continued for 3–4 weeks. For longstanding infections, several courses of treatment may be necessary.

Toxic and side effects. Foreign proteins may be released from the bodies of the dead micro-filariae and cause allergic reactions, such as fever, rashes, headache and joint-pains. Treatment does not usually have to be stopped if they occur.

Suramin

Proprietary name. Antrypol.

Dose. 500 mg–1 g intravenously once a week for 5–10 weeks.

Actions and uses. It is used in the treatment of filarial infections due to *Onchocerca volvulus* (blinding filariasis). It is also used in the treatment of trypanosomiasis.

Toxic and side effects. It is liable to produce albuminuria and casts in the urine. Nephritis and anuria are serious complications. Dermatitis, conjunctivitis, vomiting and peripheral neuritis sometimes occur.

Antimony Sodium Tartrate

Dose. The drug is given by slow intravenous injection three times a week. The first dose is of 30 mg. The dose is increased by 30 mg at each injection up to a maximum of 120 mg. The course is continued until at least 1 500 mg have been given (13 injections).

Actions and uses. It is used in the treatment of schistosomiasis (bilharziasis).

Toxic and side effects. Nausea, vomiting and coughing may occur. Like other antimony preparation (antimonials), it has a toxic effect on the muscle of the heart.

Sodium Antimonyl-Gluconate

Proprietary name. Triostam.

Dose. 190 mg by slow intravenous injection.

Actions and uses. It is used in the treatment of schistosome infections. Treatment is given daily for 6–12 days.

Toxic and side effects. It is less toxic on the heart than is antimony sodium tartrate.

Stibophen

Proprietary name. Fouadin.

Dose. Intramuscular or intravenous injection of 1.5–5 ml daily (or at longer intervals) until a total of 45–75 ml has been given.

Actions and uses. Stibophen is a preparation of antimony used in the treatment of schistosomiasis (bilharziasis). Intensive 5-day courses of treatment are sometimes given. That it can be given by intramuscular injection is sometimes convenient.

Toxic and side effects. It is less toxic than antimony sodium tartrate.

Lucanthone

Proprietary names. Miracil D, Nilodin.

Dose. 500 mg–1 g.

Actions and uses. It is used in the treatment of schistosome infections by *S. haematobium* and *S. mansoni*. It appears to act by preventing the formation of the eggs. It is given twice a day for 3 days.

Toxic and side effects. Nausea, vomiting, abdominal pain, dizziness and depression can occur.

43 · Drugs for Amoebic Dysentery

Emetine Hydrochloride

Dose. 30–60 mg daily by subcutaneous or intramuscular injection for 6 to 10 days.

Actions and uses. This amoebicide, an alkaloid of ipecacuanha, is used for the treatment of amoebic dysentery, amoebic hepatitis and amoebic liver abscess. It is more effective in acute than in chronic dysentery. To kill amoebae in the intestine, emetine-bismuth-iodide or di-iodo-hydroxyquinoline are given by mouth at the same time. Emetine is not given by intravenous injection because of its toxic effects on the heart.

Toxic and side effects. Prolonged administration can produce degeneration of the heart-muscle, renal damage and peripheral neuritis. It is contra-indicated when any of these conditions are present. A painful swelling may occur at the site of injection.

Emetine Bismuth Iodide

Other name. E.B.I.

Dose. 60–200 mg daily for 12 days.

Actions and uses. This, a combination of emetine with bismuth iodide, is given by mouth in the treatment of amoebic dysentery and of carriers of the disease. It may be given at the same time as other amoebicides are given by injection, e.g. emetine.

Toxic and side effects. Nausea and vomiting can be produced. To prevent vomiting it should be given in enteric-coated pills, i.e. pills which are not digested until they reach the intestine.

Phanquone

Proprietary name. Entobex.

Dose. 150–300 mg daily in divided doses for 10 days.

Actions and uses. It is an anti-amoebic drug with actions and uses similar to those of emetine hydrochloride. It can be used in the treatment of acute and chronic amoebiasis and in the treatment of amoebiasis of the liver. It may be given with emetine hydrochloride or instead of emetine and bismuth iodide. A course of treatment does not last longer than 10 days; a second course may be given at least a fortnight later.

Toxic and side effects. It can produce nausea and vomiting, and to prevent this it should be given with meals. The urine may go dark, but this is not important as it is due to the excretion of harmless breakdown products of the drug.

Di-iodohydroxyquinoline

Proprietary names. Diodoquin, Embequin, Floraquin.

Dose. 1–2 g daily in divided doses for 20 days.

Actions and uses. It is an amoebicide given by mouth for chronic amoebic dysentery. It is not very effective when given by itself and is usually given in combination with other amoebicides.

Toxic and side effects. It can cause gastro-intestinal upsets, pruritus ani, boils, and slight enlargement of the thyroid gland.

Acetarsol

Other names. Acetarsone, Stovarsol.

Dose. 60–250 mg.

Actions and uses. It is an arsenical amoebicide given by
mouth for the treatment of amoebic dysentery, usually
in combination with another amoebicide. It is also used
in the treatment of yaws.

   The same drug is used in pessary form for the
treatment of trichomonas infections of the vagina.

Toxic and side effects. Given by mouth, it can produce
gastro-intestinal upsets, urticaria and erythema. It is
contra-indicated in patients with liver or kidney disease.

Diloxanide Furoate

Proprietary name. Furamide.

Dose. 500 mg three times a day for 10 days.

Actions and uses. It is used in the treatment of amoebic
dysentery when a person without symptoms is found
to be passing cysts in the faeces.

Toxic and side effects. Flatulence can occur.

44 · Anti-malarial Drugs

Anti-malarial drugs are used in three ways:

1. Proguanil hydrochloride
   Pyrimethamine

   To suppress attacks of malaria; a person takes the drug regularly while in a malarious district, so that if he is bitten by a malaria-carrying mosquito he does not develop the disease.

2. Amodiaquine hydro-chloride
   Chloroquine sulphate
   Quinine di-hydro-chloride
   Mepacrine methane-sulphonate

   To treat a person suffering from an attack of malaria.

3. Primaquine phosphate

   To treat a person who after leaving a malarious district has the organism in his tissues and is liable to develop malaria.

Amodiaquine Hydrochloride

Proprietary name. Camoquin.

Dose. 400–600 mg daily for 3 days.

Actions and uses. It is an anti-malarial drug, used in daily doses for 3 days to stop an attack.

Toxic and side effects. Rare.

Chloroquine Phosphate

Proprietary names. Avloclor, Resochin.

Dose. As a suppressive: 300–500 mg once a week.

Actions and uses. It is used to suppress malaria. By killing the parasites it can prevent a person bitten by a malaria-carrying mosquito from developing malaria. It should be taken weekly while the person is in a malarious district and for three weeks after he has left the district.

The same drug is used in the treatment of amoebic abscess. It is also used (in doses of up to 1 g daily) in the treatment of rheumatoid arthritis and discoid lupus erythematosus.

Toxic and side effects. Gastro intestinal disturbances, pruritus and headache may occur. More serious toxic effects are oedema of the cornea, degeneration of the retina, a temporary psychosis, muscle weakness (which improves on stopping the drug) and myopathy.

Chloroquine Sulphate

Proprietary name. Nivaquine.

Dose. Treatment of an attack: 800 mg, followed by 400 mg daily.

Actions and uses. It is used to treat attacks of malaria caused by *Plasmodium vivax*, *Plasmodium falciparum*, and *Plasmodium malariae*.

It can be used in the treatment of amoebic disentery, rheumatoid arthritis and discoid lupus erythematosus.

Toxic and side effects. Similar to those of chloroquine phosphate.

Hydroxychloroquine Sulphate

Proprietary name. Plaquenil.

Dose. Treatment: Initial dose 800 mg; followed by 400 mg 6–8 hours later; followed by 400 mg on each of two successive days.

Actions and uses. It is an anti-malarial drug, active against attacks caused by *P. vivax*, *P. falciparum* and *P. malariae*, used to treat acute attacks, but as it does not affect organisms when they are within red blood cells, it has to be combined with other anti-malarials. Some organisms are resistant to the drug. It has been used in the treatment of *Giardiasis* in doses of 200 mg three times a day for 5 days.

The same drug is used in the treatment of rheumatoid arthritis and systemic lupus erythematosus.

Toxic and side effects. In the above doses it is well tolerated and much less toxic than chloroquine phosphate or sulphate.

Mepacrine Methanesulphonate

Dose. 120–360 mg daily by intramuscular injection.

Actions and uses. It is given by intramuscular injection for the treatment of severe malaria in adults. It is not used to treat children.

Toxic and side effects. It may stain the skin yellow.

Primaquine Phosphate

Dose. 15 mg daily for 15 days.

Actions and uses. It is used to destroy the malarial parasite in the tissues of people who have returned from malarious districts and might be liable to develop attacks of malaria.

Toxic and side effects. In 'primaquine-sensitive' people it can produce intravascular haemolysis, which is characterized by abdominal pain, bilious vomiting, fever, a redness of the urine, and jaundice. These 'primaquine-sensitive' people (who belong to the dark-skinned races) have a congenital abnormality of red blood cells, a particular enzyme being absent. The same effects can be produced by other drugs, e.g. acetanilide, sulphonamides, sulphones.

Proguanil Hydrochloride

Proprietary name. Paludrine.

Dose. As a suppressive: 100–300 mg daily.
    Treatment of an attack: 100 mg three times a day for 10 days.

Actions and uses. It destroys the malarial parasites (*Plasmodium falciparum, Plasmodium vivax*) in the tissues as well as in the blood. As a suppressive it should be given once a week while the person is in a malarious district and for three weeks after he has left it. As, when it is given alone, a resistant strain of the organisms may survive and cause attacks of malaria, it is often given in combination with pyrimethamine.

Toxic and side effects. There are no serious toxic effects when the above doses are given.

Pyrimethamine

Proprietary name. Daraprim.

Dose. As a suppressive: 25 mg once a week for adults.
6.25 mg once a week for children under 5 years.
12.5 mg once a week for children 5–15 years.

Actions and uses. It is used as a suppressive of malaria.
It acts by interfering with the metabolism of the
parasite. As it is tasteless, people – especially children –
are willing to take it. It may be given in combination
with chloroquine in order that any resistant strain can
be dealt with. It is sometimes used to treat attacks, but
as it is slow to act it is not very good at this.

Toxic and side effects. There are no serious toxic effects
with the usual doses.

Quinine Dihydrochloride

Dose. 300–600 mg by slow intravenous injection.

Actions and uses. This is the only preparation of quinine
in use today. It is given by intravenous injection in the
treatment of severe cerebral malaria. It should not be
given intravenously to small children, to whom it has
to be given intramuscularly in a dose of not more than
5 mg per kilo body-weight.

Toxic and side effects. Mild toxic effects are ringing in
the ears, deafness, giddiness and tremor. Permanent
deafness and blindness have been caused by large
doses of quinine. Blackwater fever may be produced in
P. falciparum infections.

45 · Drugs for Trypanosomiasis

Pentamidine Isethionate

Dose. Prevention: 300 mg every 3 to 6 months by intramuscular injection.

Treatment: 150–300 mg daily for 12 to 15 days by intramuscular injection.

Actions and uses. It is used to prevent and treat trypanosomiasis. It is not effective in severe advanced cases with involvement of the central nervous system, for which tryparsamide is used. It is also used to treat leishmaniasis.

Toxic and side effects. It can produce hypoglycaemia. A painful swelling may be produced at the site of the injection. The drug is not usually given by intravenous injection as it can then cause a serious fall of blood-pressure (for which adrenaline and methyl-amphetamine are antidotes).

Melarsoprol

Proprietary name. Mel B.

Dose. 3.6 mg per kilo of body-weight by intravenous injection daily for 3 days.

Actions and uses. It is an arsenical trypanocide used in the treatment of severe case of trypanosomiasis due to *T. rhodesiense* and *T. gambiense*, especially when the nervous system has been invaded by the organism. It is advisable that treatment should be given in hospital. A second course of treatment should be given after an interval of 10 days. Children are given half the adult dose.

Toxic and side effects. Acute febrile reactions can occur. The drug can produce arsenical poisoning, especially of the brain.

Suramin

Proprietary name. Antrypol.

Dose. Prevention: 1–2 g intravenously.

Treatment: 500 mg as first dose, followed by 1 g weekly intravenously for 5 weeks.

Actions and uses. It is used for the prevention and treatment of trypanosomiasis infections.

Toxic and side effects. The kidneys can be damaged and albuminuria be produced. Vomiting, diarrhoea, dermatitis and peripheral neuritis can occur.

46 · Drugs for Leprosy

Drugs for leprosy can be given singly; a combination of anti-leprosy drugs is not indicated as there is no evidence that bacterial resistance is thereby delayed or prevented.

Dapsone

Other name. D.D.S.

Proprietary name. Avlosulfon.

Dose. 25–100 mg weekly by mouth or intramuscular injection or 25–100 mg weekly, increased to 200 mg weekly.

Actions and uses. It is an anti-bacterial drug and the most effective of anti-leprotic drugs, but treatment has to be continued for several years. After the skin lesions have disappeared, maintenance doses may have to be given for at least eighteen months. Dapsone has also been used for toxoplasmosis and dermatitis herpetiformis.

Toxic and side effects. Anaemia may occur, for which iron should be given; for severe anaemia a blood-transfusion may be necessary. An acute dermatosis can be caused and require treatment by anti-histamines. Hepatitis can occur. An acute psychosis can occur, but it is not certain whether this is due to the drug. Severe reactions suggest that the dose of the drug be reduced or the drug abandoned. Dapsone can be given during pregnancy without danger of harmful effects on the fetus. It should not be given to patients with kidney disease.

Solapsone

Other name. Solapsonum.

Proprietary name. Sulphetrone.

Dose. 1–3 g daily by mouth; or 0.25 of a 50 per cent solution twice weekly by intramuscular injection.

Actions and uses. It is an anti-bacterial drug given by mouth or intravenous injection for all types of leprosy. It is similar in its actions to dapsone. Treatment has to be continued for months or years.

It is also used for dermatitis herpetiformis.

Toxic and side effects. When given by mouth, it produces the same toxic effects as dapsone but they are usually milder and less frequent. Given by injection, it can produce a slight dermatitis.

Clofazimine

Proprietary name. Lamprene.

Dose. Varies with body-weight, activity of disease and response to treatment. For patients with leprosy of recent origin 100 mg 3 times weekly; for patients with bacilli resistant to other drugs 100 mg 6 times weekly.

Actions and uses. It is an anti-leprotic drug used for all forms of leprosy. It can be used for previously untreated cases, for patients who are intolerant of other drugs, and for patients with bacilli resistant to other drugs. In the acute inflammatory stages of the disease it can produce rapid relief from fever, pain, nerve-swelling, etc., and cortico-steroids (if being given) can be reduced in amount or gradually withdrawn.

Toxic and side effects. Epigastric discomfort and diarrhoea can occur. High doses given for a long time can produce a harmless reddish discoloration of the skin, grey-biue pigmentation of the lesions and a discoloration of the urine; all these discolorations disappear when treatment is stopped.

Thiambutosine

Proprietary names. Ciba-1906, SU 1906, DPT.

Dose. 500 mg daily, increasing to 2 g daily in divided
doses.

Actions and uses. Treatment is continued for several
months or years. Resistant strains of the organism
may develop after a year of treatment, and when this
happens other drugs have to be used. A preparation is
available for intramuscular injection once a week.

Toxic and side effects. None known.

Dirophal

Proprietary name. Etisul.

Dose. 5 ml twice or three times weekly by inunction.

Actions and uses. It is used for cutaneous leprosy, being
rubbed into the lesions. Resistant strains of the
organism may develop. To prevent this, ditophal is
given in the early stages of treatment in combination
with an anti-leprotic drug by mouth.

Toxic and side effects. Sensitization of the skin can occur.
When this happens, the drug is discontinued for 3
weeks. If sensitization recurs, the drug is not used again.

Rifampicin

Dose. 450–600 mg daily as a single dose on an empty
stomach.

Actions and uses. It kills leprosy bacilli in the skin in 5
weeks and is effective against dapsone-resistant bacilli.

Toxic and side effects. Nausea, abdominal discomfort, a
skin allergy, and orange-red discoloration of urine and
skin can occur.

47 · Miscellaneous Drugs

Adrenaline

Dose. 200–500 mcg by subcutaneous injection.

Actions and uses. Its actions resemble those produced by
stimulation of the sympathetic nervous system. It
increases the rate and output of the heart, constricts
blood-vessels, relaxes the muscles of the bronchi,
reduces the movements of the gastro-intestinal tract
and bladder, and produces glucose from the liver-cells.
It is given by injection in the treatment of asthma,
status asthmaticus, and acute allergic conditions.

It may be combined with a local anaesthetic to prevent
its absorption and localize it (by its constricting action
on blood-vessels) and so to prolong its effect. To stop
bleeding from capillaries it is applied locally in a 1 in
5 000 solution. It may be given in a spray to reduce
swelling of the nasal mucous membrane.

Toxic and side effects. It can produce palpitations, tremor
and anxiety. It is contra-indicated by hyper-thyroidism,
heart-failure, and in anaesthesia by cyclopropane,
halothane, and tri-chlorethylene.

Calcium Gluconate

Dose. 1–5 g by mouth; or 1–2 g by intramuscular or
intravenous injection.

Actions and uses. It is given to provide calcium in states
where there is a calcium deficiency, which increases
muscular and nervous excitability with the production
of tetany and sometimes fits. Calcium deficiency can
occur in parathyroid gland deficiency, chronic renal
disease, rickets, coeliac disease, idiopathic steatorrhoea,
and uraemia.

Dicyclomine Hydrochloride

Proprietary name. Merbentyl.

Dose. 10–20 mg.

Actions and uses. Many of its actions are similar to those of atropine. It is used to relieve gastro-intestinal spasm, peptic ulcer, ulcerative colitis, biliary or renal colic, and dysmenorrhoea. It is given as a syrup for infant colic.

Toxic and side effects. As it increases intra-ocular pressure, it has to be used cautiously if the patient has glaucoma.

Disulfiram

Proprietary name. Antabuse.

Dose. During test period: 500 mg–2.0 g twice daily.
   Subsequently: 500 mg daily.

Actions and uses. It is used in the treatment of alcoholism. By itself it produces no symptoms, but if a person who is taking antabuse takes any alcohol he develops severe symptoms (due to the formation in the blood of acetaldehyde). These symptoms include flushing, raised pulse rate, palpitations, nausea, vomiting, and a feeling of constriction in the throat. In the test period the patient takes antabuse for 2 days, and on the third day he takes both antabuse and alcohol in order that he may experience the effects of the two together. He then takes a dose of antabuse daily – in the knowledge that if he takes any alcohol at all he will become acutely ill.

Toxic and side effects. Death from cardio-vascular collapse has occurred during the treatment. Demyelination of motor and sensory nerve-fibres has caused peripheral neuropathy.

Hyaluronidase

Proprietary names. Hyalase, Rondase, Wydase.

Dose. In units as determined.

Actions and uses. It is an enzyme which enables injected
fluids to permeate tissues more readily. It is used to
increase the diffusion of electrolytes when given by
injection, to increase the absorption from an intramuscular injection of diodone (used in x-ray examination of the renal tract), and to promote the absorption
of fluids injected subcutaneously in infants.

Aprotinin

Proprietary name. Trasylol.

Dose. 500 000 KIU by slow intravenous injection,
followed by 200 000 KIU 4-hourly by intravenous
infusion.

Actions and uses. It inhibits the actions of several
proteinases, including trypsin. It is used in the treatment of acute pancreatitis and the fat embolism
syndrome, and prophylactically in doses of 200 000
KIU before and after upper abdominal surgery.

Toxic and side effects. Hypersensitivity reactions can
occur. Penicillins, tetracycline, gentamicin, cephalo-
sporins and chloramphenicol should not be mixed
with it in the same infusion bottle as they are altered
by it.

Chenodeoxycholic Acid

Other name. CDCA.

Proprietary name. Chendol.

Dose. 10–15 mg per kilo body weight daily or 1 000 mg daily.

Actions and uses. It is used to dissolve small radiolucent cholesterol gallstones. Symptoms should be mild enough to permit up to 2 years' treatment. It is best used for patients who are old, have severe cardio-pulmonary disease, or are otherwise unfit for surgery.

Toxic and side effects. Diarrhoea is common and usually responds to temporary cessation of the drug or reduction in dose. The drug is contra-indicated for women who might become pregnant and when symptoms and signs of gallstones are prominent.

Neostigmine Methylsulphate

Proprietary name. Prostigmin.

Dose. 500 mcg–2 mg by subcutaneous or intramuscular injection. 15 mg by mouth.

Actions and uses. It prolongs the action of acetylcholine, a chemical substance formed at the terminations of some fibres of the autonomic nervous system. It is used in the treatment of myasthenia gravis, the injections being repeated when necessary. It is used (because of its action in stimulating plain muscle) to treat post-operative paralytic ileus and urinary retention, and to expel gases from the intestine before x-ray examination of the kidney, ureter and gall-bladder.

In a 3–5 per cent solution it is applied to the eyes to reduce intra-ocular pressure of glaucoma.

Toxic and side effects. It can produce intestinal colic. Atropine sulphate (1–2 mg by subcutaneous injection) is the antidote.

Propantheline Bromide

Proprietary name. Pro-Banthine.

Dose. 45–90 mg daily in divided doses.

Actions and uses. Many of its actions are similar to those of atropine. It is used to reduce biliary or renal colic, to reduce sweating and salivation, and to reduce secretion from the gastric glands and the movements of the intestine.

Toxic and side effects. As it increases intra-ocular pressure it has to be used cautiously if the patient has glaucoma. It should also be used cautiously in patients with pyloric stenosis or enlargement of the prostate gland. Big doses can cause a dry mouth and blurring of vision.

Azathioprine

Proprietary name. Imuran.

Dose. 2–4 mg per kilo of body-weight per day.

Actions and uses. It is used in tissue-transplantation as it suppresses the immune-response to a transplant. It is used in conjunction with prednisolone or actinomycin. Treatment is given continuously.

It is also used in auto-immune states and has been used in haemolytic anaemia, systemic lupus erythematosus, polyarthritis nodosa, ulcerative colitis, Crohn's disease, and acute and chronic polyneuropathy, rheumatoid arthritis and the nephrotic syndrome.

Toxic and side effects. If nausea, loss of appetite, and bone-marrow depression occur, the drug is stopped or the dose reduced. It should not be given to patients with liver disease, for liver damage has occurred.

Methalone

Dose. 100 mg daily.

Actions and uses. It is a steroid drug, a synthetic derivative of testosterone, used to reduce the amount of cholesterol in the blood. Treatment has to be continued for several months.

Toxic and side effects. None reported. It does not cause masculinization.

Emepronium Bromide

Proprietary name. Cetiprin.

Dose. 100–200 mg in the evening; dose reduced when effective.

Actions and uses. It is an anti-cholinergic drug with actions on the tone of the bladder-muscle, increasing the capacity of the bladder and delaying the sensation of fullness. It is used to treat incontinence and 'irritable bladder', and following operations on bladder, prostate and urethra.

Toxic and side effects. There are no serious toxic or side effects. It has to be used with caution when the patient has glaucoma.

48 · New Drugs

This and the following page are left blank so that the nurse may add information on new drugs produced after this book was published.

New Drugs

Index